You, Me and the Space  Between Us

Matt Davies
MSc (Tavistock), UKCP, MBACP (Accred) UKAHPP
(Accred), COSRT (Accred), ISSM
Matt is a marriage counsellor and psychosexual and relation-
ship therapist, who trained at Tavistock Relationships and
has worked in two NHS settings.

Sarah Davies
Sarah is a movement and somatic coach, trainer, and a
founding member of Open Floor movement practice.

Matt and Sarah Davies blend therapeutic techniques with
movement in workshops on sexuality and relationships. They
see clients together in relationship therapy sessions as well as
each having their own practice in London and Sussex.

Matt and Sarah Davies

You, Me and the Space Between Us

How to (re) build your relationship

Lagom

First published in the UK by Lagom
An imprint of Bonnier Books UK
4th Floor, Victoria House,
Bloomsbury Square,
London, WC1B 4DA

Owned by Bonnier Books
Sveavägen 56, Stockholm, Sweden

facebook.com/bonnierbooksuk/
twitter.com/bonnierbooksuk

Trade Paperback – 9781788708142
Ebook – 9781788708159
Audio Digital Download – 9781788708166

A CIP catalogue of this book is available from the British Library.

Designed by Envy Design Ltd
Printed and bound in Great Britain by Clays Ltd, Elcograf S.p.A.

1 3 5 7 9 10 8 6 4 2

MIX
Paper from
responsible sources
FSC® C018072

Lagom is an imprint of Bonnier Books UK
www.bonnierbooks.co.uk

To Ry. May life be full of love.

Contents

Part 3: BUILDING EROTICISM AND LOVE IN THE SPACE BETWEEN US

Introduction

To love and be loved. Isn't that what we all strive for? The mark of a life well lived? We hope to flourish and be nourished by our relationships, particularly our most intimate ones. Love is effort made in good will. It is willingness to look at the other in a positive light, to see underneath the behaviours that might irritate you. It is readiness to understand their personal difficulties and struggles in life, hold the light for them when they cannot find it themselves. When we start a new relationship, we take a step into the unknown. We don't know where this partnership will lead us. Love is a process and a practice.

The structure of a relationship is what gives us possibility: possibility for a life lived together in love, fun, fullness, and satisfaction, of belonging with another or others. Relationships can be made beautiful through the structure that contains them. When we commit to love in a relationship, we open to the possibility for chemistry, balance and reciprocity between the partners. At times, the rhythm might be off, and issues might take work to resolve – that is what makes the relationship authentic, honest, and alive. When the harmony aligns again the relationship is even more satisfying.

The structure of the relationship keeps us going, bidding us keep trying when we come to an impasse. It allows for mistakes to be re-written and our creativity to be employed in more ingenious ways in forging a bond with each other. There are often two sides, or two ways of looking at it. On the one hand our partner can inspire us with visions and desires, full of potential of intimacy. On the other hand we have the realisation that making the relationship align with our vision is far more difficult than we at first thought. The structure of a relationship is necessary to build love.

When lovers get together, the combination of two people catalyses a third quality that cannot be created by either individual alone. When things are going well, we find our partner's idiosyncrasies charming and amusing. We can accept and manage all kinds of behaviour because we have a store of goodwill and resilience. There is a sense of ease, of being tuned in and empathic to each other's internal worlds. We feel noticed and valued, intimately connected to one another. The erotic charge is alive and well and we feel sexually fulfilled. In these moments, we might see through the fog of day-to-day troubles to the inner nature of our partner behind it all. We can remain curious and interested in their feelings and thoughts and we feel understood in the whole context of our life, including work and family. We are attuned to one another and to feeling loved and being loving.

But when uncomfortable emotions – frustrations,

disappointments – are not expressed, we spiral downwards, turning to things for distraction: over-work, addictions and other diversions. These things may be done without deliberate intent. Serious tensions might involve contemptuous and deprecating remarks, betrayal, affairs and even bullying behaviour and emotional or physical abuse.

It is inevitable and natural that the bliss of connection is broken at times. Whether through our own actions or someone else's, there are moments when we fall out, fall down and fall apart. In such moments we are disappointed, holding onto the expectation of constant harmony. Disappointment is one of the most difficult emotions to experience. It is painful, humiliating and frustrating. Through disappointment we are thrown back into ourselves and feel alone and isolated. Speaking about it renders us vulnerable and exposed. The sexual charge is eroded and passionate couples become flatmates.

Modern relationships bring certain trials. We are all subject to the distractions and difficulties of living in the twenty-first century, where partners are sometimes struggling to keep themselves, their relationships and their families on track. The notion that we have to get everything from our partner produces stress. Each has to be lover, best friend, advisor, confidant, playmate and, for some, co-parent. It's a tall order to fulfil all these roles.

In years gone by, marriage was an economic arrangement of family stability. Is the vision of a long-term commitment unrealistic, unobtainable and undesirable? Is it a relic from another era? Is it boring? An oppressive institution? Does it inhibit our natural adventurousness and quest for the new? Nowadays, we can meet a partner by swiping on our phones and equality between the sexes has levelled the playing field – so why bother staying together? Traditional relationship models – heteronormative, monogamous, involving marriage and children – are shifting and changing. There are many different ways to have a successful relationship: LGBTQ+ couples, polyamorous folk and child-free couples demonstrate that relationships don't have to follow a traditional model to be fruitful and rejuvenating. There are many different kinds of loving, long-term relationships to explore.

There is more freedom today to be the people we want to be and to express our gender identity and sexual preferences with far more acceptance than in previous decades. But with more choice and freedom comes greater expectation that we should be able to get what we want out of life and our relationships. Couples and families, and the individuals in them, are continually evolving; sometimes we and our external structures take time to catch up.

There is no single model for a successful intimate relationship. Relationships are dynamic and fluid, constantly in flux, and people are complex. Each person has their own emotional signature with unique needs and desires at different times and in different situations. As well as relating to each other, we are also constantly in relationship to ourselves and our personal inner world of thoughts, feelings and impulses. There are rhythms and cycles to relationships because people change and adapt themselves to each other. As each partner evolves, the relationship's capacity for growth is sometimes stretched and tested.

Everyone in relationships will have their own expectations of what the relationship means to them. At times, there will be disappointment at the way you are treated or responded to by your partner, resulting in lost connection. Sometimes these moments are minor, but they still represent a 'falling apart' to some extent. Unmet expectations, desires and requests will often surface in irritation or anger. You may fight, retreat or close down, depending on the dynamics of your position. It is often in love, sex and intimacy where the most conflict in relationships can arise because these areas are of such vital importance to our overall wellbeing. But it is what you do with conflict that matters.

When things are bad enough for long enough, couples will seek help in relationship therapy. Often it is one partner pressing for it and the other isn't fully on board. For some people, seeking advice is shameful and admitting defeat, so they struggle on from one crisis to another, while bitterness sets in. Research shows it can take as long as six years before they reach out. But there are also couples who see therapy as an important aspect of their lives. Seeking help early offers the best chance for recovery.

Who is this book for?

You, Me and the Space Between Us: How to (re)build your relationship is for all couples – new couples, old couples and tentative couples; unhappy couples and happy ones. It offers a practical and useful handbook to every couple in all kinds of relationships – including traditional marriage, same-sex marriage, civil partnership, ethical non-monogamous relationships and open or polyamorous relationships and free unions. Relationships may be co-habiting, long-distance or online, both sexual and emotional. Marriages can be love marriages, or arranged marriages. Whatever form of relationship you are in, there will be inherent difficulties. However, societal prejudice and discrimination add another layer of complexity for those couples who do not fit the mainstream model.

With this multiplicity of arrangements for pairing it is no surprise that often things can and do go wrong. And the fact is, relationships are always a challenge. In the metaphor of the relationship as a dance, sooner or later your partner will step on your toes.

What you will learn in this book

In this book, we travel through the journey of an intimate relationship from its early beginnings when we first fall in love to the point where the relationship can sustain and grow this love. We provide you with the building blocks and the tools to create and sustain a loving, growing and sexually vibrant relationship. We use stories from the people we have worked with, as well as examples from our own relationship. Though our clients' stories have been anonymised and elements altered to protect the identity of the individuals. In each chapter, we provide exercises to help you practise and embody what you have learned.

The first part of the book, 'Two People Coming Together', covers the intoxicating but sometimes confusing beginnings of a relationship when we feel attracted to another person, perhaps even fall in love, and start a sexual relationship. You will understand what happens when you are attracted to someone and why this starts to fade after a while. You will become aware of the pitfalls of this intoxicating experience and how to avoid them. You will learn to navigate the sometimes confusing experience of sex and desire. We will look at the ideas and beliefs that we absorb from culture and our upbringings that create difficulties and confusion in this area. The book will help you transform the way you think about sex and desire, leading to easier and more satisfying sexual encounters.

The second part of the book, 'The Building Blocks of the Relationship', begins at the point when the couple makes some kind of commitment to creating a relationship. That is when we actively start to build the relationship and co-ordinate our lives to make space for each other, draw boundaries and make agreements about how we will do things together and be with each other. This is the stage when communication comes to the fore in all relation-ships – and when most disagreements and breakdowns in communication occur.

We show how and why communication breakdown and disruption occur in key areas of every relationship, the main factors that lead to relationships falling apart and how repairs can be made more quickly before things get out of hand. We explain how it is indeed possible to change negative impulsive reactions into positive thoughtful responses. We guide you through common communication mistakes that couples make and help you transform a breakdown into a breakthrough, as well as looking at creating boundaries, managing boundary transgressions and avoiding affairs.

In the last part of this book, 'Building Eroticism and Love in the Space Between Us' we show you how to build a relationship that can thrive. In these final chapters, you will learn about the 'third body': the place between you where you meet, learn about each other, navigate difficulties and move through differences. We show you how to identify the third body and how to nourish and grow it. You will find out about the importance of being able to move away from and towards your partner so that you can maintain your identity in the midst of a loving relationship where you can also be together as one, and how to regain your spark of eroticism and sexual connection. You will learn that your own development and growth are part of the growth of the relationship. Finally, we will show you that all of this is in service of building a love that can be sustained for the good of each of you as individuals, the relationship, and beyond.

Why we have written this book

As a couple who work in the field of relationships, this book shines an extra-sharp light on our relationship. When things are going well, it is glorious; we feel like we know what we're doing and we've got our act together. When things are going badly, it's humiliating; all our techniques, our hours of training, therapy, self-development, facilitating workshops, being supervised and offering sessions for other couples seem to amount to little. And now, there is more at stake: the longer our relationship, the more precious it becomes. The more we put ourselves out there as relationship 'experts', the more painful the potential of our relationship blips – 'We should know better.' 'If we can't help ourselves, how can we help our clients?' After the self-criticism, we go to our toolkit and one of us will make an intervention. And luckily, something has always worked. We reach out; we have experience, hope, resilience and commitment.

One of the questions we ask ourselves is: how can we dare to show up for each other? Can we be courageous enough to reach beyond the barriers between us, the defences of fear and judgement that we have built up over time? Love is a mystery, a powerful bond that ties our lives to those of others. How can we live knowing we have loved enough and loved well? How can we live in love so that our love can be a force for good?

These questions have been part of our journey and this is why we have written this book. We have learned from our personal ups and downs, our dark days of misery, our own heartbreak. We've had times of really hating each other and times of distance, when we may as well have lived on different planets, without any curiosity for the other and their inner life. And then just regular times of bickering, low-level fighting, not bad enough to do something about it, but just a moany, grumpy, slightly grouchy kind of relationship, where we didn't know how to improve it.

We're having more fun now than we did in our twenties. Yes, we have arguments, disagreements, hurt and upset, but we're more skilled in how we deal with them. We play well and find the funny side of things more easily. We are more agile with our disputes and commit to working through them. As each of us changes, which inevitably happens, the relationship changes – it has to. We emerge as new people, and these new people are in our relationship. We want to show readers how they can live more loving lives.

There have been leaps in research on how relationships affect us on every level; physically, emotionally, mindfully and spiritually, which makes now an exciting time. This relates to embodiment. Embodiment focuses on how the body is felt from within, along with a 'felt sense' of the human experience. It is the ability to experience ourselves as physical beings, who can be 'touched' at an emotional level. Embodiment is an awareness of the body and an emotional and mindful alignment with that awareness. This comes from the premise that our bodies, as body psychotherapist Nick Totton says, 'skillfully respond to complex, subtle, contradictory information and unconscious material'. Embodiment is a rich and complex sensation, but also an elusive nonverbal experience and hard to describe.

So much contemporary living revolves around technology, which usually takes us away from awareness of the body. As the time we spend on screens increases, we can be disconnected from relationships because we can be disconnected from our bodies, and vice versa.

A note on the case studies: composite stories

This book contains many stories and case studies from our clinical practice. All names and identifying details have been changed to protect privacy. In most instances, descriptions are composites of many cases which have been simplified to reflect general concepts and approaches.

PART 1

Two People Coming Together

Attraction and Our Search for 'the One'

'To say that one waits a lifetime for their soulmate to come around is a paradox. People eventually get sick of waiting, take a chance on someone, and by the art of commitment become soulmates, which takes a lifetime to perfect.'
— CRISS JAMI

Choosing 'the One'

Sometimes love appears completely irrational. When you first meet and fall in love, everything can seem perfect: you are compatible, at ease; you feel seen, heard, supported and loved. However, as time goes on, in any relationship, you will encounter problems. In times of crisis, it is easy to ask ourselves, 'why this person and not that one?', when years down the line, we see our partner with all their faults, as they see ours. When you are not getting along, it is tempting to wonder, what if you had chosen differently? Would this be happening if your partner were someone else?

Could you have chosen anyone? Could any of your former partners, or 'might-have-beens' be your partner instead, had the circumstances been different? Don't many of us share plenty in common, enough that we'd be a good enough fit? Of all the billions of people in the world, how do we choose one for us? Is your somebody the special one, or just the person who happened to be there, at the right time? If your relationship has reached a stalemate, it is easy to wonder if you might be happier elsewhere, with someone else.

Every relationship reveals aspects of ourselves. These aspects will only change as we take responsibility for them, not when we switch one partner for another, or try to change our partner into a new version of themselves. Whoever you choose will highlight qualities of yourself that you'd rather not see.

Forming a connection

Choosing a partner is sometimes instinctual. We might get a feeling about them quickly, perhaps a spontaneous spark or connection. In other situations, there can be ambiguity and doubt – it might take a while to warm to each other. We might spot them across the room or we see pictures of them on their dating profile and something piques our interest. Maybe we're not sure what exactly. But we get a hunch; our curiosity keeps drawing us to them. They seem different to others and we feel an affinity with them. There is a familiarity, even a feeling we've met them before.

Now we start to fantasise. We imagine all sorts of things very quickly. Our selective vision, rose-tinted glasses are working beautifully. We see them as special. We want to meet them, to be met by them; we feel the longing for contact. This longing for union leads to desire. Desire starts to grow inside us.

The honeymoon period

The beginning of a romantic relationship is called the 'honeymoon phase'. It is epitomised by the aching love, the pull to see the loved one as much as possible. Each person becomes unique and special to the other. Everything they do is charming and wonderful; we delight in their movements and the way they talk; the sun comes to shine on our life. So we give ourselves over, surrender to the fantasy of meeting 'the One'. We let down our defences and open ourselves up to let them in. Suddenly the world appears differently to us because we have allowed ourselves to experience more than our usual self-centred view of it. This expanded sense of the self feels blissful; all our senses are awakened. We literally *feel* more. The world appears richer and more vibrant to us: colours are brighter, food tastes better, the sunset more meaningful and even a grimy railway station is beautiful. We often feel a wonderful merging with the one we love and want to share this amazing world with them. For some people, sexual experience can feel like a divine union of souls and bodies, where the self seems to disappear.

Sexual desire lights the fire of curiosity. It magnetises and draws us towards the apple of our eye. It can electrify the space between us such that the other can *feel* our attention. Attraction is a kind of intrigue and lovers create infectious energy through mutual passion. Erotic fantasy can become obsessional. This is the frenzy of 'falling in love'.

Desire can take us to the moment of decision that our new lover is 'the One' – the one I have been searching for, the one to make me whole. Other factors can also take us to this moment of commitment, including religious or social expectations which we may feel compelled to comply with even if we feel ambivalent. This decision to commit to a relationship means that we act on our desire to make it happen.

When desire is congruent with our thoughts and feelings, and impulses and our felt sense of ourselves, we just know something is right within us. This means we can fully enter into a commitment with joy and confidence. It is my desire that brings my will into union with my thoughts and feelings; it reaches across the space between us and touches us both inside. Desire is will that carries us towards an imagined future, from now to 'then'. Desire is filled with hope. It is the force of human will, when we can go through any sacrifice for our beloved. We have hope and faith and trust.

The dynamics of sexual attraction

When we look for a partner we are often looking for someone with similar values and lifestyle to us; we want to feel understood and safe so we seek compatibility and we measure that by shared beliefs and interests. These are often the elements which we use to select a partner. But underneath that, there is also some kind of intangible pull that we don't fully understand. When there is a sexual aspect to this, that is the thing we are usually most aware of. There are many reasons why you might be attracted to a partner – similarities or differences can be attractive.

When we find ourselves sexually attracted to someone, the forces of polarity are often at work. Polarities create a charge between two people because of the pull of opposites. Sometimes you may not be aware of what it is that is attracting you; at other times, you may notice something in them that is attractive and that highlights your deficiencies in a way you hadn't been aware of before. For instance, you notice that your new love interest is very tidy and ordered around their home with a minimalist simplicity around them. While you are more chaotic, living among a creative plethora of things. You are inspired by their approach to life, you make efforts to tidy up and they to loosen up. You think this person is the perfect match for you partly because they have something you don't. They can bring zen into your life, that quality of order that you didn't know you were missing and now want so much. They are amazed at how relaxed you are and find your happy-go-lucky arty existence utterly charming. They want some of that in their life.

A polarity is, by definition, informed by its opposite. You cannot have one without the corresponding polar opposite of it. They define each other. In the above example, chaos is defined by order. Where one person is ordered, their polarity is also present – there may be elements of disorganisation in their person, too. Polarities operate within each individual person. We are all managing our own range of internal conflicts within us: between charming and grumpy, frivolous and serious, extravagant and thrifty, gregarious and shy, courageous and timid, rigid and fluid, superiority and inferiority, benevolent and malevolent, joyful and sad. We are likely to prioritise one side of these polarities, which determines the conclusions we come to about our personality. This bias would have formed from experiences in our early lives, as a healthy way of surviving in a family system. An ordered person may have grown up in a chaotic household, for example, and so chose to develop more order as a way of making sense of this turbulence. The person who grew up in a strict or controlling environment now lives with lots of things around them in a more loose, liberal way, to make sense of the authoritarian influences of the past.

The beautiful thing about attraction in relationships is that it pulls those underdeveloped or unacknowledged aspects of your own polarities into your life. This creates a charge between two people that literally feels magnetic, because it is. The polarities of your qualities are pulled together. It is also true that similarities in character can create an exciting magnifying effect, where each partner is mirrored. You see a reflection of yourself in the other and it is enticing. At the beginning of an intimate relationship, there is an incentive to display the favourable characteristics that attract you to each other because the charge of the polarities and mirrored similarities generate electric feelings between you. You instinctively know how to maximise your qualities that are attracting them. We want to be who they think we are. At first, this is easy because we are focused on the rewards. It is a perfect reciprocal relationship and very gratifying for both. We have fallen in love. We sense this person is a perfect match.

Revealing our blind spots

At the beginning of a relationship, partner choice is often made initially for unconscious reasons, driven by the attractive pull of polarities, as we have explained above. But other forces are also at work which are all related to each other. The most important of these are projection and splitting.

Projection is the process of misinterpreting what is

inside as coming from the outside. In the beginning of a relationship, projection creates strong attraction because we project our internal idealised image of a lover onto the partner and believe they really are perfection personified. Splitting is another word for acknowledging only one side of a polarity, as explained above. We split off the unacknowledged half of the polarity and project it onto our partner. For instance, someone who cannot own their own anger may split it off and project it onto their partner.

In the early stages of a relationship, as the polarities pull us towards another and we begin to project all our fantasies onto them, we create an interactive web of positive connections between us. Then there comes a time when we consciously choose them. For some people, this is the moment they realise their partner is 'the One'. At this stage, partners make a commitment and choose to love and adore one another. But at times of relationship breakdown, there is a reversal and they become 'the One' to blame, to hate and vilify. In such moments, anyone else can seem far more attractive.

When we come into a relationship, we see a reflection of ourselves in the other. We love their kindness, sense of humour, passion, for these are also parts of us that they hold a mirror to. We see in that mirror that they share our outlook and we feel validated and good around them, making us want to be with them. But as the relationship matures, you may see a reflection of yourself you don't like, akin to looking in a wonky mirror as in an old-fashioned fairground. It can be difficult to see an image of yourself that you were not aware of. This is natural. We simply can't see ourselves unless we have the mirror of our partner to look in. This can cause conflict because in our distress, we can blame our partner for our own faults. But this is the power of relationship, to bring awareness to our blind spots. We can only get a full sense of ourselves in our relationships with others, romantic or otherwise.

SHARON AND MEL

'Why weren't you there for me?' Sharon has been extremely unwell and is recovering from a recent illness. Sharon criticises her partner, Mel, for not knowing what she, Sharon, might need and for not caring for her in the way she would have liked. Mel is frustratedly saying how she tried to do what Sharon wanted, such as making food she thought Sharon would appreciate and getting the magazine Sharon usually enjoyed. But it wasn't enough, wasn't quite right. Sharon felt let down and disappointed. Specifically, she was annoyed that Mel didn't take much initiative and seemed unconfident in caring for her. She thought the magazine choice lacked creativity. While they argue, the space between them feels empty and neither can see the situation from the other's viewpoint. In the frustration of the problem, Sharon exhales deeply and tears roll down her cheeks as she speaks further about her fears of illness. During her illness, she faced mortality and reached the point of reassessing her life, which shook her. The level of vulnerability it took her to has shaken her. She realised she had been trying to fit into a 'people pleasing' version of herself and feels resentment around many of her relationships. She had been going through a tough patch and was at a low ebb; instead of getting in touch with her own vulnerability, she blamed Mel.

It is often easier to externalise a conflict than own it in ourselves. We pick a fight with our nearest and dearest to avoid our sense of vulnerability. Instead of falling apart internally, we create a situation where we fall apart externally. When two people form an intimate relationship they create a rich interaction, which can either create a virtuous cycle of beneficence or a spiral of negativity at times of stress. Sharon projects onto Mel a lack of creativity and of taking the initiative, and yet this is the very quality that Sharon is feeling vulnerable about in herself. It can be helpful at moments like this, when we are pointing the finger, blaming, criticising, condemning, to ask ourselves: what is it about me that notices this in you? Do I, for example, see you as annoyed, but actually, it's me who is annoyed but I don't want to feel it, own it, or take responsibility for it? Am I projecting my anger? When it's hard to be me, I criticise you, or I drink, smoke, shop, gamble, work or go online. The irony is that to be with you, I need to tolerate my discomfort of being me.

Healing through the relationship

Through the power of projection of our idealised other, we seek emotional healing from childhood wounds – someone who will love us completely and unconditionally and make up the inevitable deficits from imperfect parents and carers. These wounds might be overt or very subtle. No one gets through childhood unscathed; parents and carers always fail some of the time, no one can be constantly attuned to us. It is necessary for growth to learn how to manage loss of connection and regain it.

Matching internal ideals and other unconscious motives forms an attraction which pulls partners together. Initially, there needs to be enough similarity for us to understand each other and enough difference for us to be interested. But people are complex; this adds to our intricate, mysterious beauty. When two people come together this enigma increases. In the same way of baking a cake, where the different ingredients interact with each other, so too each individual in a relationship brings their particular flavour and nuances that add to the overall outcome. The cake might rise to its full spongy, delicious potential or it may deflate into a flavourless disappointment. In any relationship, both are possible, sometimes simultaneously.

GLADYS AND SEAN

Gladys and Sean were instantly attracted to each other. When they met it felt like they had met each other before; they shared a similar humour and had so much in common. Years later, they discover they have similar childhood wounds. They were not aware of the similarity of their wounds, they just knew they felt like a good fit. Gladys had a strict controlling father; she developed a vigilance to constantly monitor his moods and a way to separate from her own needs that didn't get met. She would 'escape' into fiction and films and lived in a world of story. Sean had a mother who abandoned him by moving to another city and leaving him with his aunt when he was young. He remembers crying in bed at night and then having to harden himself emotionally to protect himself from further hurt. Their similarity was that they were both cautious about making emotional connections to protect themselves from further potential hurt. When Sean gets scared of being abandoned he appears aloof and withdrawn, which reminds Gladys of her father before he would get angry with her. When she can't read Sean it signals danger, which makes Gladys pull back from Sean in fear and distance herself from him, which in turn makes Sean feel even more scared of being abandoned, which makes Gladys feel more unsafe, and so on and on in a negative cycle. When Gladys is absorbed by the arts and culture that she so loves, Sean feels abandoned, which triggers his young, painful feelings of being left.

Gladys and Sean are implementing protective strategies learned in childhood that actually no longer serve them. In fact, their strategies are scaring each other and amplifying the problems between them. When they can see what is happening they understand what they really want from each other: healing and reassurance. Now they learn to disclose what is happening for them emotionally and to communicate by using their voices to ask for what they would like from each other.

The illusion of the perfect someone

The idea of a soulmate is alluring. It means there is someone out there meant only for us and us alone. This romantic view is presented to us through countless films and literature, from fairytales to *Romeo and Juliet*, and, more recently, by Disney and Hollywood. Again and again, we see stories based on searching for our soulmate who we either unite with or, in star-crossed destiny, spend our lives yearning for.

Research by psychologist C. Raymond Knee found that people who believe in soulmates also believe that people either 'click' and are meant to be or they don't and should move on. At the beginning of the relationship, they can be intensely passionate and satisfied with their partners, riding on an emotional high while things are good. However, when problems inevitably arise, they often don't cope well. As anxiety arises, they tend to end the relationship and seek the next 'true' match elsewhere.

Knee also found that people who don't believe in soulmates mainly look for someone who will work and grow with them, resolving conflicts as they arise. They tend to be less intense, passionate and satisfied with partners at first. However, they are motivated to look for resolutions to conflict and stay in connection with their partner. Their relationships tend to be longer and more likely to grow over time into something more satisfying.

Overall, this research shows us that we need to be able to commit to resolving issues as they come up if we want a stable, long-term relationship. That may require us to be challenged, to change and to accept that we are not 'the perfect one', just as our partner isn't either.

We have to take responsibility for choosing our partner. Not because they are our destiny or they complete us in some way, but because we decide to commit to them and to the growth work it takes to have a satisfying relationship. We do this not just because they happened to come along but because we created them as 'the One'.

The idea of finding a soulmate, as much as we might

yearn for that and however beautiful the idea, is, in real life, detrimental to the quality of relationships. The expectation of a 'happy ever after' is not realistic and leads to disappointment and disillusionment. When couples with a more 'romantic destiny' mindset are with someone they consider to be their soulmate and encounter difficulties, the relationship is less likely to survive than those with a 'romantic growth cultivation' mindset who see relationships develop over time.

As relationships develop

As you get to know one another better, you begin to see a more nuanced, complex portrait of your partner, including those characteristics or behaviours which are more difficult, less attractive and harder to respond to. The relationship enters a new phase in which the differences between you might create conflict. We talk more about this in Chapter Six.

Now, the initial positive characteristics that attracted you begin to shift to the polar opposite. The partner who puts effort into being ordered starts finding it tiring to do this for the other person. They begin to let things go, becoming more chaotic at times. The partner who revered this orderliness in the other is now disappointed. But similarly, they become tired of holding the polarity of being 'happy-go-lucky'. They can be grumpy and short-tempered at times because they are worrying about finances and work goals. And likewise, this produces a shift in the other.

If the polarity doesn't shift internally within each person, then it becomes fixed between the couple and the magnetic charge reverses: those things that once attracted the partners to each other now repel. The orderly person is now viewed as rigid and uncompromising. The chaotic, happy-go-lucky person is seen as a hopeless failure with no ambition. This is why couples can start out feeling joyous with each other and then later fall out in frustration and fury. This can then force a shift of awareness to balance the polarity within each individual.

Most of us imagine we are exempt from the cliche that 'love is blind' but after a year or two, shifts unavoidably occur in the relationship and our blinkers fall away. Researchers have found that after 18 months to two years into a relationship, the 'honeymoon period' comes to its natural end. Our projections and fantasies come crashing down, perhaps leaving us feeling slightly disillusioned. Our lover appears not to be the person we had initially hoped. The things about them that used to charm and intrigue us become irritating and they fail to meet our expectations. Something goes wrong, the mask slips and the person underneath is revealed. That's when things can unravel. Disappointment hits. 'Oh no, this person is not the person I thought they were. Have I made a terrible mistake?' We start to see our partner in a different light, more objectively. The rosy tint of our spectacles fades and we begin to notice their self-centredness, stubbornness or laziness. These too are parts of us that we have denied or disowned, but once the filter is removed, we readily notice and get irritated by them in our partner.

When two independent people come together and form a relationship, difficulties are bound to arise. It would be unusual if this didn't happen. Their different histories, values, outlooks and psychic make-up create a rich interaction of processes which catalyses both a cycle of bounteous loving and, at times, triggers a spiral of negativity. Transitions in the individual and in life bring about movement and change which is inevitable, unavoidable and inescapable. We all have these make-or-break moments, when either the relationship ends or the work of building the relationship begins.

Our story

We were in our late twenties when we first met, both of us willing and available for a relationship. Sarah delighted in Matt's sociability and Matt appreciated Sarah's sense of adventure. We had a slow beginning of our intimate relationship. As we fell in love we enjoyed the build-up of tension and expectation; holding back was a way we communicated the seriousness of our feelings. This wasn't a fling: we weren't going to rush.

We embarked on a huge adventure, taking a month off to go travelling. We packed our rucksacks and our guidebooks. We were in a love bubble, unworried by trials like an out-of-date passport suddenly discovered at the airport. The world looked glorious through our rose-tinted glasses. Problems dissolved into fluid resolutions; these were carefree, exciting times. We had only been together for a few months but were confident this was a meaningful journey with this significant person at a serendipitous time of our lives. Initially, the trip was great. We were in harmony, agreeing on what to eat, how to travel, places to visit. We clicked, joked and played. We revelled in the sense of being intrepid explorers, not only of the outward landscape but also inwardly, enraptured in each other's attentions. However, about halfway into the trip, minor irritations surfaced.

There was criticism of small selfish behaviours: taking more than their fair share of food, being slightly pushy in wanting to go to yet another market, not getting out of bed in time to get the bus without having to rush. We saw parts of the other we didn't like and felt feelings neither of us wanted to feel. It was disappointing. The niggling thoughts started to creep in: is this person actually inconsiderate? Egotistic? Manipulative? Materialistic? Have we been deluded? The edges started to fray, the charm started to wear thin, the thrall began to wither. We were miles away from home, away from our support systems (this was before mobile phones so also out of reach and out of contact). The strain broke into petty arguments, the atmosphere between us was flat, we were ill-equipped to manage ourselves or each other, neither of us had the ability to talk about it. The dream trip became a bit of an endurance. A new expectation was dawning – the thought that as soon as we were home we would split up.

Exercises

This is the first of several exercises throughout this book that you can do to help you build and rebuild your relationship. We've structured them so they make a coherent journey. You have picked up this book so we're going to assume you are looking for new ways to manage in your relationships. We highly recommend the exercises to help you actively do that. Each has helped us, and continues to help us, in our own relationships and with our clients. They are tried-and-tested and they work.

Most of these exercises take two people. If you do want to try the exercises but your partner doesn't, it is possible to modify the exercise, either to practise on your own or to try with friends; it doesn't have to be with your intimate partner. We give suggestions for how to do it on your own. Our take on it is that if one of you changes in the relationship, the relationship changes. If one of you is doing something different, the dynamic cannot be the same. It only actually takes one of you to change to make the relationship different. And, then, everything has its time.

Quite early on in our relationship, Sarah was recommended *Passionate Marriage* by David Schnarch. She read it and was amazed by how it spoke to her and some of the issues she was having with Matt. She recommended Matt to read it and bought him his own copy. It sat in his 'pile of books to read one day' for ten years. During that decade, she implored him to read it. In the meantime, she digested the material in the book and it infused their relationship in many subtle ways. Eventually, the day came that Matt read the book – he loved it! He developed a voracious reading habit for books about relationships (and then started the long training to be a couples' therapist). So, if your partner is as keen as you are to embark on this journey into your relationship, that's wonderful. And if not, we hope that this story can help you relax into knowing everyone has their own time.

Calling them 'Exercises' may make them seem like hard work. There is a risk that they sound time-consuming and require lots of effort. Alternative terms for them might be 'playtime' or 'suggested focus' or 'experiment'. Some of them are communication exercises, others are exercises designed to increase embodiment, the ability to 'read' and have awareness of the body. Embodiment requires attention to sensations, to the physical felt sense of experience. Like growing muscles, this increases with practice: it will be beneficial to repeat these exercises as many times as feel of interest to you. We know that a slight challenge can sometimes feels satisfying, which is our intention by offering you these, but if it feels like a big leap or too much effort maybe it's not the right time, or the right exercise, for you right now. Feel free to put it aside for another time and to pick and choose as works for you. Or, if you're raring to go and want to get stuck in, then please do.

Appreciations

This first exercise is called 'Appreciations'. This one is a simple start, but the most important ground of the relationship. Appreciation of your partner is the most common aspect that can get lost in the busyness of life. We start to take each other for granted. It's so important to feel appreciated by your partner. A little word of gratitude goes a long way. Not only that but countless studies have shown that we feel better within ourselves when we make an effort to notice the positive things our partner does.

On the simplest level, this is as straightforward as saying something to your partner that you appreciate about them. But for it to carry more weight, it should be specific, giving a particular example with a time and place when you noticed it and felt grateful. For instance, instead of saying, 'I appreciate you are a caring person', you could point out when your partner displayed caring behaviour, such as:

'I appreciate that you brought me a cup of tea in bed this morning.'

'I appreciate watching you have fun when you play ball with the dog.'

'I appreciate that you fixed the cupboard this afternoon.'

'I appreciate the kindness you showed me when I was unwell.'

Linking it with a specific behaviour makes it more tangible for your partner, rather than something more vague or general.

We recommend three appreciations, every day. You might save them up and say them all at once or as they arise. Count them, make a mental note to yourself. Less than three isn't doing this as an intentional practice and more than three can end up diluting them. A continual stream of appreciations might seem like a good idea but then they lose their power and feel thin.

The common responses to the idea of giving your partner three appreciations every day include:

'What if I run out of things to say?'

'What if we're having a difficult patch or there's lots of conflict and I can only think of the things I don't appreciate?'

'What if I'm appreciating my partner and they don't appreciate me?'

'But that doesn't seem challenging at all, I'm sure we already do three or more appreciations without even realising we're doing it.'

One of the more obvious benefits of the 'Appreciations' exercise is that you are carving out a specific time to give the appreciations and you are holding them in mind to deliver at this time. As a receiver, it feels lovely. We feel seen – 'They noticed that the other day!' We feel valued – 'They saw that it mattered.' And we feel acknowledged –

'They communicated that it meant something to them.' All this goes towards establishing trust and building warmth.

One of the benefits for the giver that we only get to experience after a while of this being a practice is that we are taking more notice of the things we appreciate. This increased observation, purposefully looking out for something you appreciate, also feels good to the giver. So, if you are doing this on your own, don't underestimate the subtle powers of seeking out the things you appreciate. Giving three appreciations as a daily practice fosters kindness and develops a culture of gratitude and respect. We ward off resentments and criticisms by creating a 'bank' of goodwill and high regard.

You might mix up the way you say them:

I appreciate how you . . .

I really liked it when you . . .

Thank you for . . .

Sometimes, we have lots of appreciations for each other and other days, when things are strained, it feels impossible to think of even a tiny one. On those days, use your powers of attention to notice something, anything; maybe broaden your peripheral vision and use your creativity. In times of hostility, even attempting to do this exercise can shift the cold barriers that can grow in an impasse.

Try the exercise as we have outlined it and if it works for you then great – use it for as long as it continues to work for you.

NOTE: If your partner doesn't want to do this with you, you can write the appreciations down in a journal and give the appreciations to yourself.

2

Navigating Sex
and Desire

Sex, desire and arousal

Creating and maintaining a loving and sexually alive relationship is the central task of being a couple. At the beginning of a romantic relationship, sex and love follow us into the bedroom. We feel sexually attracted and in love. Sex can be an effortless expression of our feelings of love for each other. We feel nourished with loving attention and satisfied through sexual contact.

Inevitably, over time, this sense of abandon and effortless pleasure begins to fade. The sex becomes less exciting, more infrequent and perhaps even unappetising. Unspoken resentments and ideas about what should or shouldn't be happening in our sex life may begin to surface, leading to possible discord, affairs and break-ups, some of which may come from deep sense that there is something is wrong, which we perhaps project onto our partner.

Sex and sexual desire (the feeling of wanting to have

sex) are among the most confusing areas of modern life to navigate. We carry with us many ideas and beliefs from childhood, and from our own culture, about sex and desire. For example, what the purpose of sex is, what good sex should look and feel like, and how often we should be having it. These are largely unquestioned beliefs that exist outside of our awareness and yet they play a profoundly important role in how we engage with this area of life. Understanding where these ideas come from, and some of the feelings that get attached to these ideas, will help us to navigate this complicated area of life with our partner. First, let's look at how we understand the terms sex, desire and sexual arousal.

Sex

We define sex as any sexual activity that is intimate and sexually arousing. This can include kissing, caressing, attending to each other's bodies, touching in ways that are intensely pleasurable, in a private or relaxed atmosphere, and having amorous or romantic conversations. The depiction of sex as penetrative intercourse that has the aim of orgasm is highly heteronormative and exclusionary – there are many ways for sex to take place which don't include penetration nor have orgasm as the goal. The aim is pleasure, connection and lovemaking. This can be enjoyed in a vastly broad variety of creative ways, which often involve mutual touch of the genitals but doesn't necessarily have to.

There are also other categories of sex which we do not talk about in this book. For instance, there is digisex, where partners engage in sexual exchanges online. There is also autoerotic sex and self-pleasuring or masturbation, where someone engages in solo sexual activity.

Desire

Desire is the emotion of longing, yearning or wanting. It is an impulse or a craving and the motivation that pulls us towards contact like magnets pull towards one another. The impulse, the motivating force, is different depending on whether your desire is spontaneous or responsive.

The standard narrative is that normal healthy desire happens spontaneously – a person feels desire arising in them like a drive, a need. They have a thought that comes up out of the blue, or a sensation like an itch, and then desire sex to satisfy it. It's what's often portrayed in the movies – a sudden ignition of passion. But the definition of normal healthy desire has been broadened and redefined. Sexologists and researchers have shown that another healthy way of experiencing desire is responsive desire, sometimes called contextual desire. A person is already in a sensual or sexual situation, in the right conditions and circumstances, and *then* they feel desire. This doesn't mean they have any deficiency in any way, they just have a responsive desire style. Some people will recognise themselves as veering towards one desire style or the other and many people will recognise themselves in both.

Desire for sex is motivational. We may feel desire for sex because we are motivated by feelings of longing to be emotionally connected with our partner, to enjoy physical contact with them or satisfy needs for acceptance and self-esteem. Once there is enough motivation for sex, then desire can be felt. The sexologist Rosemary Basson has shown that if there is motivation to engage in sex, that can lead to desire arising during sex: motivation precedes desire.

Arousal

Sexual arousal is the feeling of being turned on, which usually happens when we feel sexual desire. We are responsible for our own arousal. We create our partner as sexy and erotic by focusing selective attention to those things which turn us on about them. We also project our own erotic fantasies and ideals. When things get difficult in your relationship it can mean you stop focusing your attention and fantasies and start noticing negative aspects instead.

However, arousal can happen in the body even when we don't feel desire. It is called 'non-concordant' arousal. Or it might happen that arousal happens in the body when the person doesn't feel desire. Our body acts out of alignment with our feelings and there is a disharmony – our body is doing one thing and we're thinking or feeling another. We might be feeling disgusted but having all the bodily reactions of being turned on. Or the other way around: we're feeling desirous but nothing is happening in our body, there is no reaction. Non-concordance can be very confusing and frustrating. The body doesn't always respond in the way we want it to. There are a multitude of reasons, including physical problems with the body, alcohol or drugs, or psychological reasons such as ambivalent feelings about the motivation for having sex, anxiety, fear or stress. We are indebted to Emily Nagoski for her writing in this area.

In this chapter, we talk about common beliefs that create problems in sexual relationships, especially in the early stages of a relationship. We talk more about sex and desire in a long-term relationship in Chapter Nine.

Common beliefs about sex and desire

We live in a world where sex is everywhere: in advertising and movies which draw us in to watch polished sexual images, scenarios and innuendo in advertising, music videos, computer games, films, TV, social media and, of course, easily accessible pornography. Sex is an industry which most of us buy into every day. The messaging we get from this media informs how we think about sex, how we feel about sex and our sexual behaviours. What we experience and how we are treated in our early sexual forays adds more to our sexual templates. For many, sex is complex and may not immediately convey the idea of pleasure. For others, sex has acquired mythical standards that are difficult to meet in reality, giving rise to unrealistic expectations and performance anxiety. But despite these differences, the main ideas and beliefs we have about sex and desire – what it is, how to do it and what it (and we) should look like – we have acquired unknowingly. We have identified five of these common beliefs that we think are the most important, though there are probably more. These ideas can create an enormous amount of pain and confusion as we try to navigate our sexual desire, the sex that we want and the sex that we have.

Sex is a performance

Sex is often thought of as a natural function of the body: a bit like eating, it's just healthy to want it and enjoy it. The whole of nature does it in one way or another. But in humans, sex has been raised to the level of an erotic art, taking it beyond a natural act and into the realm of drama and performance. This creates confusion, and we can get caught in the objectification of sex and override our own feelings and sensations. Unlike their parents and grandparents, children and young people of today have the internet to find answers to their sexual questions. But this can often lead to unhelpful and misleading information and ideas about what sex is supposed to 'look like', which is increasingly informed by porn.

Heterosexual sex is often portrayed by actors with idealised bodies, depicting a dominating male, driven by lust, who can seemingly endure unending intercourse without ever ejaculating. There is little or no verbal dialogue or eye contact between partners. The woman reaches orgasm through penetration, which is rare in reality for most women unless there is clitoral simulation as well. Women are also shown as experiencing spontaneous desire, when research shows this is true for only 15 per cent of women. For the majority, their desire is responsive. This portrayal of women and sex is driven by male fantasy and is unrealistic. In this way, most of us already have ideas about sex from pornography or other sources before we have a sexual experience with another person.

The influence of the porn industry on our sexual lives is huge. Porn movies and actors convey unrealistic and stylised messages which many people take as the standard to be achieved. These depictions and activities are limited to what is culturally accepted to be sexually desirable, feeding us the message that if we don't look sexy, we're not worthy. To perform successfully, we need to have the right body shape, or acquire it by working out, going on a diet or having surgery and cosmetic procedures. We are sold sex and we buy sex: the right clothing to be seductive and attractive and the lotions and potions and make-up so we look sexy. With sex all around us, we are fed a message that if we don't look 'sexy', no one will want us. But looking sexy is very different from being sexy – being able to enjoy the sensations of sexual contact and arousal.

Research shows that young people are having sex in ways that are determined by what they watch in porn. Each individual develops sexual styles: sexual styles characterise what they find arousing and exciting. The sexual style defines the imagined lover, the specific attributes that spark their desire, how they are aroused and what is done together in sexual scenarios to produce all the flavours of sexual pleasure. We must please each other, take care of our partner's pleasure, arouse them and perform for them. This can create performance anxiety, which is inhibiting to the enjoyment of sex and to the sensations of sexual contact and arousal.

We like the safety of our cultural construction of sexual activity. There is a shared 'script' for what people do sexually. This is comfortable and reassuring at times, as sexual activity can raise vulnerability and shame, but it can also detract from being present and spontaneous in sexual contact with your partner. It's also healthy to experiment out of this comfort zone and connect with our partner and pursue our desires, rather than just 'perform' the roles we've been assigned. Believing that sex is a performance is damaging to emotional contact. It can leave many people spectating their own performance in their heads, which takes them out of a real emotional and physical experience. It can also leave us feeling disappointed that we haven't lived up to unrealistic sexual ideals.

Sex is a need

There is an important distinction between needing and wanting. While desire and passion might feel like an need, physically they are wants. Desire and passion are emotions – the longing and yearning for the other. 'Needing' is usually confined to those things that we depend on for our survival. A need for a glass of water, for instance, satiates thirst and keeps the body hydrated.

Implicit messages tell us that if we're not having sex, there's a problem. We are made to feel like life is passing us by and we're missing out on something potentially rewarding, fulfilling and meaningful. We're conditioned to want sex. More than that, we are conditioned to believe that sex is a need. Sex might be desirable, exciting, interesting, captivating or seductive but it is not a physical need. We won't physically die if we don't have sex, but we might struggle emotionally if we are longing for sex and intimacy and our partner isn't willing to meet us.

But it is unlikely your partner will want to join you in intimacy, love and sex when you express that as a need. There is something passive and disempowered about needing your partner for those reasons. Neediness comes from a place of emptiness, not a place of fullness where you have something to offer your partner through your passion. Coming to sex with a deficit rather than abundance may not be perceived as sexy: it's about wanting to take rather than give. In our stressful, busy culture, someone else wanting something from us does not tend to evoke desire, rather we will likely see it as a chore. This is the problem that arises when sex is seen as a need – the other person can feel objectified and under pressure to gratify their partner's so-called 'needs'.

Yet, when our partner can reveal their hunger for emotional connection, which might be met through sexual intimacy, it can invite loving, sensual contact. This is such a delicate communication of innermost longings, and it can feel so tender and vulnerable to express. The intricate dynamics of two people with all the myriad of responses can mean it could be triggering, to feel emotionally needed, wanted and desired.

Sex is shameful

Whether we acknowledge this consciously or not, some of us may believe that sex is shameful. This belief may have been present and unquestioned in the families and communities in which we grew up. Perhaps we remember a time when we felt confused at the thought of sex and horrified at the thought of our parents 'doing it'. What we take in emotionally from our homes forms a basis for how we relate to sexual partners later on. We unconsciously take in how our parents spoke to each other, their level of shared affection and how they nurtured us. We hone our sexual scripts from what we are told or not told about our bodies, masturbation and pleasure. If our parents or carers were embarrassed to talk to us openly about sex and pleasure, we can determine falsely that such activities are shameful. If there is abuse in our history, then the feelings of shame will likely be even more intense.

To make matters more complicated, shame around sex usually lurks at the lower edges of our awareness. The nature of shame is to hide. No one wants to admit that they find sex shameful: nowadays, particularly for young people, finding sex fun and exciting is far more socially acceptable. So, we may pretend that sex is easy, fun and exciting, while simultaneously experiencing sex, and the prospect of sex, as difficult and shaming.

The goal of sex is orgasm

What is the aim of sexual desire? This is a question that is rarely given much consideration, which is curious, given how much importance is placed on the fulfilment of sexual desire. World-renowned sexologist Henry Bancroft asserts that orgasm is the goal of sexual activity and signifies its conclusion. The orgasm occupies a central place in our beliefs about sexual fulfilment, despite its brevity – the average orgasm lasts a few seconds. Many people do not derive the satisfaction they expect from sex or their orgasms. For instance, research looking at heterosexual men and women shows as many as 30–40 per cent of men believe they ejaculate prematurely. More than 50 per cent suffer from some kind of erectile disorder. Many women have difficulty achieving orgasm during sexual intercourse and some have never had an orgasm at all.

A study of heterosexual young people found their concerns around sex were focused on whether or not the female has an orgasm during sexual intercourse. The male partner felt responsible for stimulating their partner adequately, while the female felt responsible for being psychologically prepared to experience it. The authors of the study suggested there is room for more informative sex education, particularly when it is known that: a) orgasm difficulty is women's number one sexual concern in clinics; b) most do not orgasm during sexual intercourse and c) 10 per cent have never had an orgasm at all. Other women fake having an orgasm during sex, either to satisfy expectations of their partner or to bring sexual activity to a close. Suffice to say, there is a lot of hype and anxiety around orgasm and many people are labelled with a sexual disorder connected with orgasm.

Most of us do not stop to question our ways of making love. Alternatives are not well represented. Many existing ideas about sex and pleasure derive from historical ideas in Western culture about male dominance and the importance of male pleasure. For instance, it was previously believed that men have to ejaculate to remain healthy and it was thought to be women's responsibility to provide sex for this reason. This was challenged in the nineteenth century by Alice Stockham, one of the first family doctors and gynaecologists in the United States, who was an advocate for women's emancipation. Stockham brought Eastern sexual practices into modern sexology. She called her method Karezza. In this method, neither partner chases orgasm. Sexual activity was carefully cultivated with breathing practices and positions to bring about a heightened sense of being present in the moment by stilling the mind, intentionally letting the breath be audible and through eye-contact. Stockham and others avow that sexual ecstasy results from coolness and inner peace. This is contrary to commonly-held Western beliefs that the more we do in sex, ramping up tension and heat, the greater the reward.

Research in orgasm frequency during intimate sexual activity found that for men, frequency of orgasm did not vary much by sexual orientation. But for women, orgasm rates differed considerably according to sexual orientation. One study showed lesbian women experiencing most orgasms, followed by bisexual women, with heterosexual women experiencing fewest orgasms, while another study agreed that lesbian women experience most orgasm but showed that bisexual women experienced fewest orgasms during intimate sexual activity. However, this research looked for orgasm frequency and did not take into account the broader question of sexual satisfaction. Other researchers have found that couples of all sexual orientations find satisfying ways to be sexually intimate without the need for orgasm. What most researchers seem to agree on is that a fulfilling relationship translates to satisfying sex, whether orgasm occurs or not.

Problems can arise when one partner seeks the gratification of sex and is focused on the goal of orgasm in a compulsive way. In some cases, this puts an immense strain on the sexual relationship, which then becomes merely theatre where sexual scenarios are played out. Where one partner is focused solely on their own satisfaction, sexual relations decline and often the partner decides to completely withdraw from sexual activities. When the need to satisfy the urge to orgasm becomes the prime imperative and sexual impulses are followed unconsciously, the person is not free. When orgasm is a matter of choice, when the couple are present with each other and there is detachment from the outcome, sex can lead to building more connection between you.

Sexual desire is always spontaneous

We are educated to believe that sexual desire is a drive. This is a nineteenth-century view which is now discredited but it has lingered nevertheless. Desire is part of the human motivational system, and like sex, it is value-laden. Motivation towards sexual contact and sexual confidence is governed by multiple factors. But primarily, within each of us there is a dual system which either acts as a brake and inhibits us against sexual arousal or an accelerator, motivating us towards it. It's different for each individual. Some tend towards shyness and are more anxious and inhibited sexually. Others can be more brazen, and easily excited and aroused. But we all have our own brake and accelerator and use both at different times. People can swing from one pole to the other.

A large proportion of people do have low spontaneous desire, which goes against cultural messages that spontaneous desire is 'normal' and anything other is a low libido. If we don't have spontaneous sexual desire, we can be made to believe we are not normal. We all want to feel wanted by our partner, we want to know they are attracted to us, that we are their special one that lights their fire. But people with contextual desire get turned on when the right combination of factors is present. If our partner has contextual desire they may not long for us, they may not feel a sexual longing in the way we would like. For instance, it could be they need to feel emotional closeness, have an absence of stress and anxiety or be away from the home and children in order to lose themselves in sexual pleasure.

Bringing awareness to the experience of sex, desire and arousal

Asking questions about our own experience of pleasure and arousal can help us to navigate the (sometimes confusing) arena of sex and desire.

Who is the pleasure for?

An important question in giving and receiving sexual pleasure is, who is this for? Is it for my pleasure or yours? Who is doing what? And to whom? Undertaking any project successfully with another person so that both are happy can be difficult to pull off at the best of times. Think of a DIY project with your partner, like putting up a shelf or assembling flat-pack furniture – tempers can flare and then everything breaks down. But when we are talking about two people giving pleasure to each other and wanting to get pleasure from each other at the same time, there's even more at stake.

In the early stages of a sexual relationship, it is likely that one partner might be more confident and more directive than the other. Over time, a fluid reciprocity can develop. Both sexual partners may be project leaders, happy to follow what the other wants. But at the beginning of a sexual relationship, we don't always know what we want or we are not able to say it. We may feel uncomfortable and awkward talking about sex. Being aware of what you are doing and why when you engage in sexual activity, and asking who the pleasure is for, is an important first step in unpacking awkwardness in this area. This will help the relationship to develop in safety and trust can lead to more open communication and expression between partners.

How do you get aroused?

Physical arousal is experienced throughout the body, often imperceptibly at first. Initially our heartbeat increases, pupils dilate and breath quickens. But the imagination must be involved as well – we need to imagine what it is we desire. The minds of people with spontaneous desire are quick to engage in imagination and fantasy and the bodily changes might occur half an hour before the sexual activity starts. For people with contextual desire, it might be half an hour after the sexual activity has begun. Both spontaneous desire and contextual desire are OK, normal and good. The person with more spontaneous desire is usually also seen as the one with higher desire, as they tend to want sex more often, so initiate more, or complain if sex isn't happening as regularly as they want. The person with contextual desire is seen as the one with lower desire, who might not initiate so often and may give responsibility for their arousal to their partner.

Being aware that these differences exist but that, importantly, they are not an obstacle to enjoying sex with your partner, is the first step towards navigating these differences. We talk more about ways to work with differences in desire in Chapter Nine.

Where is your focus during sexual activity?

Are you there to be looked at? For your body to be enjoyed as an object? Are you there for your own sexual gratification? Social conventions around sex can turn you or your partner into a set of external attributes, with physical and objective appeal, detracting from the actual feeling and sensations you are experiencing in the body. Objectification of oneself or the other can render the person unable to sense their own body and be aware of their feelings. This can lead to coldness or disconnection, sometimes even cruelty. The space between two partners during sex can quickly become one way, where someone is acted upon for the purposes of personal gratification – for example, when one partner is focused solely on how to achieve their own orgasm – removing the possibility of anything else being experienced. The opposite extreme is to maintain our focus inwards on our bodily sensations and feelings. This can lead to alienation between partners because attention is focused away from the other.

For centuries, females have been sexualised through body image, clothing and make-up and denigrated if they do not fit cultural and sexual stereotypes. This objectification on a massive scale is so ordinary that the damage can go unnoticed. Those who grow up focused on their appearance can believe that their value correlates to the amount they please other people and conform to often impossible ideals. The corrosive influence of social media is gradually being recognised yet the damage ensues, not only for females but for all genders and people of all stages of maturity. This can undermine satisfying sex as it takes us away from feeling and sensation.

In relationships, there is healthy and unhealthy objectification. Unhealthy objectification makes the partner the source of the other's sexual arousal. This can lead to ever more pressure on the objectified partner to create sexual excitement and 'do it' for the other. This is clearly not a mutual relationship and in extreme cases can lead to loss of empathic connection, denigration, coercion, aggression and sexual violence.

The antidote to this is that each person needs to take responsibility for what turns them on, not leave it to their partner. The electric charge of sexual excitement happens when two or more people can each take from and give to the other with mutual consent. For this to happen, there does need to be a degree of 'healthy' objectification. What we define as healthy is seeing your partner as different to you, external to you and 'other' to you. This is differentiation – the recognition that you are distinct from me. This is necessary for eroticism to thrive. For there to be a sexual charge, we need to be separate from our partner and distinguish from them enough to remain curious about them, to see the particulars in them, rather than the generalities of our own pre-formed ideas about them. But the empathic and feeling connection must also be present for a mutually satisfying experience – this is partly what is missing in 'unhealthy' objectification. There needs to be a balance between sensing your partner as a distinctly different person to you and focusing on your own bodily sensations and feelings. You need to be aware that something is happening between you, and that the good feelings you have are because you are sharing them with someone else. Sensing and feeling creates the warmth and heart connection in the space between you.

Questions to ask yourself are: 'How am I in this moment with you?' 'What am I feeling and sensing?' Being attuned to yourself is the first important step of attuning to your partner. When you can do both, charge and energy can flow between you. We will return to questions of sex and desire in the final chapters of this book.

Our story

Early in our relationship, we went to an embodied sexuality workshop for couples. We joined a weekend workshop of about ten other couples, some of whom had been together a long time, some were new. Some seemed blissed-out with each other; others looked more indifferent. The workshop was about self-pleasure, getting comfortable with knowing our bodies and exploring what felt good and what didn't. It was a mixture of talking, moving and dancing as a group, and then intimate exercises for each couple to do in the privacy of our own rooms.

The facilitators explained that the sessions would include a range of different relationships, from those having a difficult time to those utterly in love. Unfortunately for us, during that weekend, we were the couple having the most difficult time. We had been trying for a baby for a while and we were beginning to realise we had fertility issues. The stress was getting to us and we felt out of place at this workshop. We had been trying to keep it hidden, we felt ashamed, but that meant that we weren't getting support around it. We talked to the workshop facilitators in the breaks, which was helpful in reducing our sense of isolation.

We found ourselves comparing ourselves to other couples in the room. Some looked very sexy and comfortable together, while we felt so tetchy and unsexy with each other. In this workshop, we were a couple who had sex, not a sexy couple. We weren't in a state of bliss. Neither were we indifferent. We later learned that indifference is the most dangerous state to be in as a couple because then there is just a vacuous space between you and you can happily drift away from each other. We weren't fighting either. Fighting is a form of glue for some couples. It keeps them together, although in a miserable state. We were somewhere else altogether. We were frustrated with our situation, yet clinging onto hope. We loved each other very much but it was difficult to keep the warmth at times because of our differences in coping.

Matt was taking the boundlessly positive, 'there's nothing wrong' approach, embodying 'everything will be OK' optimism, which grated on Sarah's more pragmatic stance, which was 'there's an issue here, we need to get checked out'. This created a kind of oscillation between closeness and distance, anger and hope, disappointment and frustration.

Being our erotic selves in this workshop was awkward because of what was going on for us. One of the exercises was for each of us to show the other how we get pleasure from our own bodies. We were asked to self-pleasure in front of each other. We had not done this before, or even considered it. It would have been a challenge at the best of times, let alone when we were conflicted. Self-pleasuring was the reverse of what we normally considered lovemaking. In this situation, we were faced with our own sexual shame, whereas focusing on each other made it easier to override shame. However, we very much wanted the workshop to 'work' on us. We wanted to change our situation and trusted that this exercise would be of benefit.

We had both grown up in fairly conservative environments when it came to sex and sexuality. We had experimented in various ways, yet we were not used to relaxed erotic environments or liberal sensual expression: this was all new to us. Given our emotional state, it was a tender and tentative experience to be with each other. It was real, and vulnerable, and exposing; there was a sweet tenderness to our willingness to show up and risk feeling ashamed, and to support each other to take this step in being seen. We learned many things in that experience – not only the logistics of how the other self-pleasured, but also that being seen in our vulnerability had allowed us to connect in a new way. When each of us could self-regulate enough to allow ourselves to be seen as a separate erotic individual, we had our own sense of agency. In trusting ourselves to tolerate our own feelings, we were safe to come into connection. We found out that witnessing and being witnessed in our vulnerability is an act of courage.

Exercises

Self-focus Exploration

We have found this exercise an essential tool to bring attention to the body and to slow down and fully experience sensations as they are felt. Often, our busy lives preoccupy us and sex can become a series of learned moves that get repetitive and mechanical. This exercise is a simple way to help you rediscover your sensuality and enquire as to how you experience pleasure. It involves taking a bath or shower, drying yourself and putting on moisturiser or body oil, and then making notes in a journal if you want to.

Set aside at least 90 minutes to two hours or more. Prepare for the exercise by buying or having a body oil or cream you really like the smell of. You will be using the bedroom and the bathroom, so set them up in a way that feels comfortable and sensual to you. For instance, you may like music to relax, soft lighting or incense.

Take a bath or a shower. Slow everything down. Soak up every moment of the experience and acknowledge to yourself what happens. So, how does the water feel on your body? How do you experience the warmth? Notice what happens in your thoughts. Are you able to stay focused on the physical sensations or do you drift off and think about other things? Wash your body slowly and pay attention to how you touch yourself as you wash. Do you scrub quickly? Where do you start? Slow it down and notice what you experience as you touch your body in all the different areas that you wash.

Do the same thing when you get out of the bath or shower and towel yourself dry. Slow it down and notice the sensation and pleasure you get from feeling the towel on your skin.

Now go into the bedroom and gently massage the cream or oil onto your body. Work gently all over your body. We suggest you don't deliberately stimulate your genitals or nipples because most of us are trained to focus on the sensations in this area and often ignore or tune out other sensitive areas of the body. If you explore the rest of your body for its sensuality, you might find there are other areas that arouse you. If you feel sexually aroused, observe which part of your body gave you that pleasure.

Look at yourself in the mirror in a loving way. Focus on those parts of your body that you like. Most of us have a negative view of our body and can feel unhappy about certain parts, like our breasts, buttocks or stomach. This is an exercise in observing and focusing on those things we do like. Find something, wherever it is. You might be surprised that you find more than you think when you isolate certain aspects and look in a loving and generous way.

Finally, if you want to, write about your experiences in your journal. What did you notice in your thoughts and feelings? How did your body respond to your touch and what areas did you find pleasurable or not? You could draw a little stick figure and mark the areas you found pleasurable to touch and how you liked the touch.

PART 2

The Building
Blocks of the
Relationship

3

Communication

'The single most powerful and transformative ingredient in dialogue is the intention to understand.'
– OREN JAY SOFER

We make relationships, but relationships also make us. Relationships help us develop and grow. This developmental stage comes after what is known as the honeymoon stage of the relationship, once the magnetic power of attraction has settled down. Many of us have been lucky enough to experience the ecstatic heights of the first falling-in-love stage of a relationship. That attractive force of falling in love appears effortless but is something we actively participate in.

But many relationships don't survive the end of the honeymoon period, when we start to see our partner in a less idealised way, and more objectively, as someone separate and perhaps foreign to us. Sex starts to become less frequent and this alone can be a signal for the couple that things are changing. Physical connection decreases along with the reassurance that touch can give us. Arguments may start to happen as each person protests this loss of connection in an attempt to regain it. At this stage, one or both partners can decide it is easier to separate. And many do, believing that the relationship was doomed from the start because they are incompatible. But for those couples who choose to commit, the work of building the relationship, and allowing the relationship to make you, begins.

Communication is the foundation of a relationship

Communication is the bedrock that underpins the structural integrity of the relationship. Everything we do, don't do, say, don't say, all our responses, reactions and actions or lack of it – it's all communication. We can't not communicate. To live among others is to communicate.

Communication is not just stringing words together in sentences. Through our body language, we reveal our conscious and unconscious emotional, physical and mental state. Tone, pitch, pacing and volume of voice, as well as body movement, overall manner, touch, posture, gestures and facial expressions are part of the language of communication. Our proximity to the other, the angle of our body, standing straight or a slumped posture tells us about the potency of the speaker. The amount we mirror and match, eye contact and gaze – they all add to how we read what the other person feels. This is paraverbal communication that says so much about us. Importantly, we are more likely to censor our words than our actions, so inconsistencies in our communication easily occur.

When we think about communication we naturally

imagine the exchanges between people, the dialogue, the back and forth of reciprocal conversation between individuals. But communication goes on inside of us as well. We have our own internal dialogue, including about what we want to say and how we think our partner will respond. This is why inconsistencies in communication easily occur. Our confidence, mood and energy are often conveyed through the style of our speech more than through the spoken message. This means we are always giving others information about ourselves, even if we are holding back on actual facts and life history. Sometimes, communicating what's most important happens without us being aware, and that may not be the ideal image of ourselves that we want present. We might want to conceal particular aspects of ourselves – for example, how nervous we are, how lonely or vulnerable or needy we're feeling. But we communicate these things anyway.

Everything we say is qualified by the way we say it, where we say it and our body language or gestures as we say it. That means when we use our voice to communicate with another person, what we say is not always what is understood.

Every conversation has a context

Different contexts can constrain or enable dialogue in multiple ways. Culturally speaking, shared meanings have become attached to different scenarios. For example, a candle-lit dinner is an invitation for intimacy, while shopping together at the supermarket would elicit a different flavour of conversation. The context for communication sets the stage for the kind of conversation that will occur.

Every conversation has a meaning that is connected to a previous similar discussion. Sitting in a car together provides a contained and intimate space but with limited eye contact, which can hamper the level of communication but also be less confrontational, which has advantages and disadvantages. Going on a walk, which involves moving the body, being free to stop or change pace and make gestures, can be liberating and beneficial to any relationship, creating a context within which more difficult subjects may be talked about.

Communication is embodied relating

We come into a relationship with our body, through which we think, feel and act. Emotion happens in the body, and we may or may not have awareness of the changing sensations of the event of the emotion or of a felt sense of an experience. The language of our body reveals our conscious and unconscious emotional, physical and mental state.

Within the sensations of the body, constant adjustments are going on to regulate our system, which affect our thoughts, feelings and behaviour. Consciously and unconsciously, we adapt to maintain functioning and equilibrium. This aspect of communication in the body is not in conscious awareness, but impacts how we behave, feel and think, and contributes to that inner knowing, to intuition. A racing heartbeat might be an indication that what we want to say is important to us or we might be fearing the response. A stomach ache might arise when we're churned up or nervous. If we have something we feel excited about we might feel zingy or bouncy.

There are so many ways in which we convey information

about ourselves to others that go way beyond what we say: the gestures we make, our mannerisms, how we move, how we dress, the choices we make and how we make and convey those choices. The things we choose to say about ourselves are just a small part of what we're communicating; the words we choose carry a lot of weight as well as the way we say them.

Communication is a creative process

A conversation is a creative process which builds as ideas are expressed, received, acknowledged and understood. In communication, we reveal ourselves and also create ourselves. For example, we don't always know what we're thinking until we start to speak. We speak, hear ourselves speaking and often, what we say does not fit the first time: it's not quite what we mean. It does not resonate with our truth. So we try again, with different words. We start to order and make sense of our own inner world of thoughts and feelings. We refine our thinking through speaking our ideas, whims and curiosities. Speaking helps us to think and thinking also helps us to speak; therefore, speaking and thinking are inextricably linked. Speech is not an encoding of ready-made thoughts. In speaking, we facilitate and accomplish thought as a gesture of the whole body.

The fundamentals of communication in intimate relationships

The need to be loved

Since babyhood, you have been communicating your needs, wants, desires, choices, preferences and interests. 'Yes' to this; 'no' to that. It's likely that some needs and preferences you had as a child were supported, while others were not. Perhaps we wanted to eat ice cream instead of vegetables, or to have the same pair of trainers as our cool neighbour, or to stay up late. Depending on the preferences of our caregivers, we might have gradually realised that what we wanted was not OK, not a good idea or not possible, and so we learned to curb our desires – or, at least, when and where not to show them. We learned that it really isn't a good idea to say what we honestly want or to show who we really are. Our intimate longings became hidden away, often from ourselves as well as everyone else and instead, we present ourselves in a way to get the approval and love we long for. The need to be loved moderates our behaviour. Our sense of value and self-worth comes from how we are treated and responded to in our early years.

We managed our longings by developing strategies, repressing feelings and behaving in certain ways in an attempt to feel safe, fit in and, ultimately, be loved. They began forming from our early years, inherited through family traditions, relating patterns, genes and derived from the reactions and judgements of others. We were conditioned into believing certain behaviour is good or bad. We learned how to be in a relationship with our main caregivers and this serves as a blueprint for later life. Decades later, the inevitable stresses in life can trigger these strategies developed in early life, but they have become so habitual that we think that's who we are.

Most of our bodily movements, gestures and mannerisms are also learned in early relationships. These create our physical memory patterns. By the time we are adults, the ways we use our body are unique to us. For instance, the way we walk, our gait, has been shown to be highly individual; it is unintentional and involuntary, it is how we naturally embody ourselves. A lot of what we communicate happens without us being aware. We put effort into presenting ourselves as secure, stable, functioning adults and try to hide our insecurities. And yet, through what we say, but even more through how we say it, we express our own embodied histories and the history of our family relationships. We say so much about ourselves from the way we move, our body holds that memory. Our style of embodiment develops through imitation or rejection of learned bodily habits. Out of a family repertoire of judgements, children shape their sense of self, and all of this comes to bear in the way we relate to other people when we become adults. This is particularly the case in our close intimate relationships.

Who is in charge

Communication can signal whether power is shared by the couple or concentrated in one partner. When both partners engage equally in the relationship, as a fair union of two different people with equal capability, this is a known as a symmetrical relationship. A contemporary or modern relationship style is symmetrical – a union of two individuals with an independent mindset. Both are self-sufficient, both are financially stable and have agency in the world. They have similar attributes and collaborate well but don't wholly depend on the other.

When there is a division of roles based on differences in ability and capacity, and/or contrasting strengths and interests, this is known as a complementary relationship. A traditional or 'old-fashioned' heterosexual relationship, where roles are considered gender-specific, is a complementary style of relationship. Here, the man earns more money and the woman does more for the children and the home. They tend to their different roles, which makes the relationship work. A few generations ago, if the wife had a career she loved, she might sacrifice it, while the husband would keep pursuing his career goals. Nowadays the same arrangement may exist with the roles reversed.

Complementary styles of communication involve one partner who likes to be in control of the exchange: they try to dominate what is being said and their style is often marked by orders, interruptions or contradictions. In most exchanges in a complementary relationship, there is a report as well as a command dimension to the message. The 'report' dimension is the objective message, the information – for example, 'It is going to rain'. The 'command' instructs the recipient on how the message is to be understood. The command element is conveyed through the tone of voice and style of delivery.

Imagine it is about to rain and a couple are leaving the house to go out. If they are in a complementary style relationship, you would probably hear one of them saying: 'It is going to rain, you'll need your raincoat.' By contrast, if it is a symmetrical style of exchange, you would hear something more like this: 'It is going to rain. Shall we postpone or are you OK to go out now?'

Complementary relationships maximise difference (I know what you need) whereas symmetrical relationships minimise difference (let's work this out together). The complementary style is where one person is leading the other or assumes authority, as in boss/employee, doctor/patient or parent/child. A symmetrical relationship is where each has equal power to define the relationship and the option to act freely and independently, as in peer to peer or adult to adult. Relationships need a balance of complementary and symmetrical styles. If partners are symmetrical all the time, this can lead to either constant debate or argument where each challenges the other. It is often necessary and efficient for one partner to lead and the other to follow, as in a complementary relationship.

Am I safe with you?

In establishing an intimate relationship, an underlying question we ask ourselves is 'am I safe?' Am I safe to be myself, safe to reveal myself? Will you still want me and love me when you know who I am? Will you love the parts of me I'd rather were hidden? Will you meet me in my vulnerability? Or will you humiliate and reject me?

Trust underlies the strength of every relationship. Communication essentially conveys trustworthiness – how much we take responsibility for our impact on each other. Do we act in integrity? Do we follow through on the things we have said? Do we conceal or reveal information about ourselves? We all need privacy in a relationship but concealment and secrecy are usually detrimental. Do we want to be fully seen by the other? Or are we afraid of being exposed?

All this adds to the picture of how trustworthy we are and how much we can trust our partner. When we can trust them and feel safe with them we are not only more likely to have fun and play but we can also recover from conflict more quickly and effectively. And the act of recovering from conflict and repairing the relationship can itself build trust. We look at this in more detail in Chapter Six, 'Conflict and Repair'.

Communication breakdown in intimate relationships

We are having difficulty communicating is the number one complaint we hear in our workshops and in the therapy room. So, what is difficult about speaking and listening? It is challenging when we don't like what we're hearing or when we feel misunderstood, disqualified, blamed or unloved. Communication is difficult when there is an expectation of a right or wrong answer; when there is criticism, negativity, anger and defensiveness; when there is disappointment, humiliation or guilt and when there is discounting, dismissing, devaluing, stonewalling and contempt. Non-verbal communication such as eye-rolling, exhaling, huffing, ignoring, sneering and a curling lip are signs of contempt that corrode relationships.

Healthy conflict

At the beginning of a relationship, both partners will usually make efforts to accommodate, please and reciprocate each other in ways that retain the illusion of oneness. Two people firmly become a 'we'. 'We think this' ,'we feel this', 'this is who we are' ,'this is what we like'. Merging gives us a delicious feeling of security and safety; we have found someone to share so much with – our twin flame, our soulmate, our other half, the one to make us complete.

We sometimes hold back from saying what we want to say because we fear the other's reaction or being vulnerable and looking weak in their eyes. Sometimes we may deliberately mask our feelings, but our body language can convey what we think and feel whether or not we are trying to hide it. Ambiguous communication happens when, for example, someone asks you a question and you say 'yes' but are looking in the other direction and have your arms crossed. Your body is saying no, but your words say yes. Our bodies convey implicit messages which might contradict the explicit message of our words. Perhaps there is something that remains hidden, either consciously or unconsciously, which is surfacing in some way. Ambiguous communication can highlight a conflict and might cause confusion for you as well as the person with you. It has usually developed for a purpose, often to bypass difficult issues and avoid confrontation. And often it is successful in these aims. When we're a bit vague – 'I'm not sure' – or delay – 'I'll get back to you' – or ask questions – 'what do you think?' – we stall or divert so that we can keep the peace, avoid conflict and perhaps also to avoid differentiation and remain merged.

Sometimes this ambiguity can cause difficulties. Double messages and smokescreens create distance and are exhausting for the person trying to decipher what is being said. For example, if you ask, 'Would you like to meet me for lunch?' and your partner, for whatever reason, can't say no or yes, and instead avoids a direct answer by saying 'maybe next week' / 'I'm not sure I'll finish work in time' / 'I don't really like that cafe', etc. then they are avoiding the answer to dodge potential conflict. But this means they take away your option to discuss what is going on.

In other communication difficulties, a question is sometimes asked to avoid making a statement that is more revealing of the questioner's inner world. In such instances, the question can leave the recipient confused as to what is really meant and required in response. They know that a simple answer won't really be enough. For instance, one partner asks the other: 'Why don't you ever call me at work?' This question sounds accusatory and is masking a statement about the questioner's feelings, which are not being voiced. The statement is: 'I often think of you during the day and would love it if you were to call me sometimes when I'm at work.'

In the early years of relationship, self-disclosure is necessary for partners to attract, but later on, disclosure can often turn to more negative aspects which will have a disagreeable effect. This is why some couples learn to avoid difficult areas that might be volatile. In this sense, limited communication can be beneficial in the short term as it keeps things stable. If you put something explosive into the relationship it can be ruinous. You don't want to rock the boat so you keep everything nice and happy, bending this way and that, editing out anything that could lead to an argument. This may work for a while, but in the long term, it creates a suffocating, miserable relationship. Ultimately, it leads to deterioration as nobody is free.

The cost of disagreeing with your partner is that you sometimes have to do things on your own, which may be an act of courage, finding your own way, being independent and standing on your own two feet. This means being able to express different views to your partner. When couples can do this, it is called 'differentiation' and is a healthy development from a more merged state earlier on in the relationship. We talk more about this throughout the book.

If you are unable to express a different view or tolerate hearing one then your partner is unlikely to express one either. Troubles fester below the surface as each person feels they are constrained in a box. The relationship will likely start to contract, becoming limited and boring.

Jumping to conclusions

Two people experience and hear the world completely differently. We may hear just a part of something and mistake it for the whole. We pick up certain words and think we have understood the whole sentence. We jump to conclusions.

For instance, we hear our partner start to speak about something and we immediately make an assessment of why they are speaking, what they are going to say, the purpose and the meaning. This is especially true if we are talking about emotionally loaded topics. In such instances, more of the message is transmitted through our tone, pacing, the timbre of our voice and body language. Conversation can easily get inflamed and spiral into bitter argument because we make assumptions about what the other person is saying. Thinking we understand the whole from hearing just a part is normal human behaviour.

We hear and perceive through the filter of our own felt bodily experience, with all our accumulated sensations, beliefs, assumptions, desires and aspirations, from which we construct our internal model of the world and make sense of what is happening around us. This bodily dimension is intrinsic to what is heard and seen. We translate what we take in and try to understand it by making meaning of it. We organise and categorise things, judging them to be good or bad, important or trivial, safe or dangerous, and so on. We are always working towards wholeness by making sense and meaning out of the thousands of bits of information coming in through our senses every second of the day. Internally and externally, the whole of our body is adjusting to our environment and regulating our responses, giving us a particular colour to our filter.

We fit all this information into our pre-existing ideas and internal working models and thereby give it an existence of its own. Each of us will make our own meanings out of events and find different ideas and models, seeing the world from our own unique perspective according to our lived experience. If you are a fish in a bowl of blue water, everything you see will appear blue. If you have a loud internal voice, you won't hear others clearly. Your partner says, 'You look lovely today,' but you may hear, 'You don't usually look so good.' Your partner says, 'Our neighbour has just redecorated their front room,' but you may hear, 'Why don't you do more to improve our house?' It is easy, if we are not careful, to project our own inward preconceptions and insecurities onto the world around us, including our relationship with our partner.

If we're not sure about what we are hearing, or we hear fragments, we can easily make up the rest to make something whole out of it, or we mistake a part of something for the whole. We need to have it make sense to us and this can mean we add to it from our own experience. If we're not sure about a person, we project onto them and our will can be so strong that we don't actually see or hear them properly, but instead through a filter of what we expect them to say. We may even have such strong assumptions of what our partner is like, from our pretext and prejudice, that they start getting fixed in their role of who we think they are.

BETH AND JOHN

'We're such different people now from when we first met,' says Beth, *folding her arms as she leans on the kitchen counter, not realising she frowns as she speaks. 'If that's such a problem, you can leave if you want to,'* John replies *curtly. Beth turns round in alarm. 'What do you mean, "leave"? You're always so mean,' she retaliates. And then the whole thing sparks up between them and they are at each other. An argument ensues that they have had many times, following a familiar ingrained route that they feel trapped inside. It frustrates them, yet they can't seem to break out of it.*

John heard Beth's innocuous comment in a charged and negative way. He has believed recently that she thinks he's not good enough and that she is unhappy with him. So when she says 'we're different people now', he hears something is wrong, that she's disappointed with him and, crucially, that she doesn't love him anymore. So instead of being curious as to what exactly she meant, he closes off with hurt and quickly retaliates with the remark about her having the choice to leave if she wants to. John projects his own worries and concerns on to Beth and her words.

Beth, on the other hand, was thinking how, over the years they had been together, their lives had expanded, they had got to know each other's friends, joined in shared hobbies, and she was appreciating all of this. Her intention was to speak positively about their relationship, yet she spoke in a serious way, which she often does when she's thinking out loud. When John replied with hostility, it immediately triggered her sensitivity to feeling that she doesn't really belong. So, instead of asking John why he responded like that, she makes a counterattack, protecting herself from the fear that he doesn't value the relationship as much as she does and that the whole relationship might be in jeopardy.

When they slow down enough to untangle what happened they can see how they triggered each other. The way we communicate, the inflection in our voices, our body language and gestures can convey respect or can belittle and undermine. Talking to your partner as an equal and respecting their autonomy is part of a relationship of mutuality and reciprocity, as opposed to a relationship of separateness and detachment.

But at the same time, it's often necessary to question your immediate conclusions, to stay curious and open and give your partner the benefit of the doubt if they trigger you.

Words vs behaviours

Approximately 80 per cent of the information we read in another person is non-verbal. Some say it might be as high as 98 per cent. When we meet another person, our senses are fine-tuned to perceive and interpret body language in all its intricate articulation. A sub-verbal conversation accompanies our verbal exchanges, either clarifying or conflicting with what is being said verbally. When our body language lines up with what we say, think, feel and do, and we meet another from a place of congruence, this engenders trust and safety and allows clear communication. When this doesn't happen, it is likely to bring about mistrust.

When Jack gets home from work, Lucy says: 'Hey Jack, I've had a really difficult day, I need to talk to you about something that happened with my boss at work.'

'Yeah, babe,' replies Jack, 'What happened? I'm all ears.' And he continued to scroll on his iPad.

To Jack's surprise, Lucy responds abruptly. 'Oh, sod it, I'll talk to you later,' she says, in a sharp tone. She leaves the room and Jack hears her calling her sister. What Jack had communicated by being engrossed in his iPad was that Lucy was at that moment less important than what he was looking at. The spoken message was 'I'm listening', yet he was making a more powerful statement about his connection with Lucy by his non-verbal actions, and this is what Lucy was receiving in his message. The way we articulate our body is frequently a non-verbal expression of our deeper feelings. Given that non-verbal communication has a heavier weighting than our words, it is easy to understand Lucy's response.

The importance of listening

'You haven't heard me' or 'you're not listening to me' are typical complaints that couples make to each other. We may have heard what they said, but we haven't responded in a way that validates or acknowledges their words. Communication builds our relationship when we can listen and respond empathically. Often what happens when we are triggered into old patterns is that we react defensively or negatively, dismissing or devaluing what our partner has said. A conversation is additive; information is integrated into new narratives that build and move along. One common problem is that we listen to reply, not to understand. We are forming our own argument or responses rather than really listening. We can ask, 'How was your day at work?' and as our partner is telling us, we're thinking of responses of what they should have done or what they could go back and do differently tomorrow. We want to give advice rather than just hear what they have to say. Or we're trying to tell our partner about a problem we have, worries about finances, or the children, or a health issue, and they respond by telling us about their worries. It leaves us feeling unheard and unable to hear them.

To listen we have to still ourselves, quieten our inner voice, focus our attention, be open to what we are hearing and be willing to understand. We tune in, orientating ourselves to what is being expressed. Like getting used to the sound of someone's voice or accent. It takes time to get into synch with them.

Listening is being aware of what is happening in the moment, and being relaxed and soft in body enough to hear. Absorbing information happens on many levels. We can hear the information, the tone of the voice and the feelings underneath. We become receptive instead of assertive. In an ideal situation, we put our own isolated needs to one side and allow the other person to express themselves fully. This is especially difficult if we don't like what we are hearing. Our judgements and internal commentary might be screaming out inside us, compelling us to interrupt and argue our own point of view or defend our case.

Clashing styles of communication

Couples often get into conflict because they have different styles of communicating. Some people know tacitly what they think and feel but are not good at verbalising. Other people speak in very precise and logical ways, where they make direct reference to something specific and there is no other meaning implied. People have different ways and speeds of articulating their thoughts into language. Some need more time than others to process the content of their inner world of thoughts, feelings and impulses, and to make a coherent delivery. Others find the right words to express themselves immediately. Some use many more words than others. There is also a difference in how people process and work with their internal worlds. Some do this quietly, mulling over things in silence. Others do it in an external way, talking a lot to understand themselves.

ISABELLE AND NICOLÁS

Isabelle leans towards her partner, Nicolás. She is bright-eyed and hanging on every word. She is so keen to understand him that he will pull back with fear, afraid he will be trapped. He is reluctant to say anything unless he is sure it is not going to incriminate him or upset her. Isabelle had unwittingly crowded the space between them, intruding on it so that Nicolás doesn't feel safe to unfold his process verbally. He has to keep it all in his head until he feels he has worked it all out and there are no holes in his argument. He is a barrister, after all, so his discretion is habitual. In his world, communicating effectively is not just a matter of saying whatever comes to mind. The net result of this caution in this marriage is a blockage.

It was slow work in the sessions until Nicolás could trust the unfolding process. This couldn't happen until Isabelle was able to stay centred in herself, allowing him time to reveal his truth.

Power struggles and the parent/child dynamic

Power struggles often show up in relationships as each person tries to define the relationship on their own terms. For instance, one person thinks it's OK to tease, even if it is a bit mocking or ridiculing, and the other protests against this, feeling hurt and diminished by it. Others seek to reinforce their sense of esteem by ensuring the other is always needing them and may play games to remain elusive and distant. More commonly, power struggles are driven by fear and the irrational thought that your identity, integrity or values are at stake if you give up your position on a disputed decision. At the source of a power struggle is usually fear and immobility: both partners get stuck. Therefore, it is sometimes called gridlock.

In the parent/child dynamic, the relationship is defined as one person being in authority over the other. Sometimes this can lead to a harmonious and loving connection and a lot of fun, where the authoritative partner is supported by the other. It works by consent. But at other times, the authoritative partner can become domineering and a sense of hostility can enter the relationship. When this happens, difficult memories of past authority figures can enter the scene and partners feel the frustration of powerlessness and sometimes fear. This is clearly anathema to a loving relationship.

JEROME AND VERONICA

Jerome and Veronica have recently renewed their passion for cycling together. On one sunny day out on their bikes, Jerome thinks he's being helpful when he says, 'If you shifted to the third chainring and dropped down a few sprockets you'd probably find these hills easier.' He doesn't hear how harsh and clipped he sounds. Veronica goes quiet, sighing inwardly and containing her irritation. For her, this unsolicited advice ruins the day. Inside, she is thinking, 'Don't mansplain this to me, I know what I am doing.' Her body responds with the weight of her feelings. She loses her stride and finds herself dropping further behind Jerome as he powers ahead.

Veronica hears an authoritative parental voice in how

Jerome communicates and this brings up old feelings of inferiority for her and the pattern in which they have been entrenched. It drains her energy and she feels distant from Jerome. Even though she knows it is useful advice, instead of hearing it as such, she hears 'you are doing it wrong, you are stupid'. Veronica feels depleted as she has told Jerome so many times that she doesn't like it when he speaks to her in this particular tone of voice. There is a specific clip to his words, a particular rhythm and speed in the way he talks that feels so familiar and so annoying. From this depleted position, Veronica finds it impossible to articulate in a way that Jerome can understand how he impacts her. He just hears her complaining, which irritates him as all he was trying to do was help her.

What Jerome has unwittingly done is define the relationship as one of parent/child. This is a type of complementary relationship. It is quite ordinary and can be supportive of a well-functioning relationship in its positive aspect but it is detrimental in its shadow aspect. We all carry internalised versions of our parents and we select partners who resonate with the positive aspects of them. But our partners also bring out their negative aspects, which is where things can get tricky. Once this dynamic has been initiated, it can lock into place like an unconscious game. It takes one person to break the pattern at any point: conscious awareness is key.

Bids for connection

When our partner doesn't behave or respond to us in the way we expect or want them to, and our strategies to manage them don't work, we might have a tendency to respond in one of two ways. One is to reach out to the other: to argue, get angry, criticise, pressure and plead. The other is to do the opposite: to defend, become aloof, close down and withdraw. These two types of response represent strategies for coping with the fear of not being loved. The person who is withdrawing is managing the perceived loss of connection by turning away from their partner to minimise the hurt. The person who is angry and critical is making a bid to mend the lost connection. Both strategies would have developed in childhood as the most appropriate way to manage the fear of not being loved at the time. The one reaching out learned as a child that reacting angrily got them the attention they needed, even if it was negative attention. The one running away had the opposite experience. Perhaps reacting angrily led to shame and further pain. They thus learned to turn away from the hurt of not getting what they needed.

When communication breaks down, it is helpful to find ways to reconnect with each other that move beyond either of these styles. We can do this by reaching out to make contact. A contact request can be anything from pointing out a lovely sunset to telling your partner about your day. It is simply opening a line of communication, however small, and asking if they are present. If invitations to connect are given consistently and accepted, the relationship will likely thrive. The relationship is doomed to fail if these invitations are turned down or not given at all. Research bears this out. Even a timely 'uh-huh' or a 'yeah' can be enough to acknowledge contact. It is vital to give and respond to bids for connection. A completed communication cycle helps keep the relationship alive and both partners feel attuned, loved and held in each other's minds.

Research undertaken by psychologist John Gottman highlights the difference that a timely response has in a relationship. Couples were monitored in their homes, microphones and video cameras recording their interactions. The research specifically investigated the details of what they termed a 'bid for connection', those moments when one partner is reaching out to the other or making a signal for attention. Their research showed how these bids for connection substantially affected the course of the relationship over the 20-year study. So much so that they could predict which relationships would stay together and which would encounter great difficulties.

Some bids for connection are overt – 'have you got time for me to talk something through?' or suggesting an early night while having a cuddle. Those are clear bids. If the bids are accepted, others will be made in the future, building a happy, healthy connection. Some bids are subtle, or ambiguous, or are made at times when we're busy or distracted. One partner could be reading the newspaper and call out an interesting piece of information to their partner, opening a line of communication which just needs to be simply acknowledged. It's not so much the information that is important, though it may be, but having the bid for connection accepted helps maintain the relationship. If there is no response, or a long delay in response, this rejection will have a detrimental effect on the success of the relationship.

Our story

We had our own experience of the parent/child dynamic which, at times, was difficult. This was a power dynamic driven by anxiety between us, which served as a way of coping. Sarah would move into a more controlling, authoritarian state – the parent role – in an attempt to lower anxiety. This would reinforce the complementary role of child in Matt, who would find safety in giving away power and not rocking the boat. It happens in most relationships. It can work well when the roles are used consciously and are interchangeable. What doesn't work is when they become fixed. Each of us could draw the other into an unsatisfactory dynamic. We would usually be unaware of these roles, but in particular instances they would be highlighted in sometimes ridiculous ways. For instance, in the supermarket one day, Matt asked Sarah if he could put some biscuits into the shopping basket. Where did this come from? We can laugh about it now and sometimes we still catch the odd moment of Matt asking for permission. At the time, though, it set up a really unsatisfying power dynamic, drawing Sarah into parent role. On reflection, we can see now that it comes in moments of anxiety, fear of getting it wrong, not wanting to take responsibility and needing approval. This state fed into the opposite position, which Sarah at times was willing to occupy, but was mostly unsatisfying and often led to conflict between us. She'd think, 'I'm carrying too much here. Take some of it off me, please. Stand on your own two feet.'

At other times, the parent/child would be triggered in another way. When Sarah's anxiety peaked, she could become critical and stern towards Matt, which would put him into compliant child mode. Matt then played to being 'good' or 'naughty' to the controlling 'parent'. She wags her finger and he bows his head. This dynamic would creep up on us: in stressful situations, one of us would make a subtle move into 'role' and it would trigger the other into responding in their 'role'. It became an entrenched and stubborn pattern, which caused resentment and conflict. But at other times, the dynamic would switch. Matt would be assertive and take the lead, and Sarah would fall in and follow. This is why these things can be confusing. At the time, it works quite well. Someone needs to take the lead in the relationship and the other follows. If you're not comfortable with that, the relationship can get bogged down in protests and resistance. But if you get stuck in a one-way dynamic, such as we did, it becomes difficult to manage.

When the dynamic gets stuck in one direction over the other it can have a detrimental impact. Sarah would ask Matt to do something – like hanging up the washing. Matt wouldn't do it, so Sarah would do it resentfully and 'tell off' Matt, and the dynamic continued. Matt saw Sarah, in her role, as bossy; Sarah saw Matt, in his role, as incompetent. Matt resented Sarah for being so controlling. Sarah resented Matt for his lack of agency. But we could not see how we were disempowering each other. This dynamic became quite toxic to the health of our relationship and destructive to our intimacy. It really wasn't sexy.

It took years to realise what we were doing. Once we knew the theory, the difficult bit was actually changing our behaviour. It was such an ingrained dynamic for us; we would slide back into it often in subtle ways, unconsciously pulling each other in, and realise halfway 'We're doing parent/

child!'. Being able to name it as it was happening was helpful and eventually we brought in humour, taking the mickey out of ourselves. Once we could laugh about it, the hold it had on us lessened. Sarah could then notice the triggers that would cause her to be critical or controlling – often there was vulnerability and a sense of insufficient support. Matt had to learn to stand his own ground, to feel himself as an adult and take a more active role in decision making. He set boundaries, telling Sarah to stop criticising him.

Relating harmoniously with each other means being conscious of the roles we adopt. It is about understanding and accepting our positions, while challenging them at the same time. When we can't meet our partner where they are, or welcome what they say or feel, we are, in effect, rejecting them. This creates defensiveness and communication breaks down. The aim during an interchange is to stay available, receptive, and aware.

Sarah realised she was making a cloaked request for support and learned to be more direct, which meant allowing herself to be vulnerable. Matt realised he was making a cloaked request for contact, which required allowing himself to feel the longing for that and to express that with more vulnerability and openness.

Moving towards an adult/adult dynamic meant being level and respectful with each other and facing problems together, side by side, instead of seeing each other as a problem or wanting the other to be the one who fixes problems. It is a dance of differentiating and merging. We differentiate and then something changes; it gets uncomfortable and we hold onto familiar rails every now and then to steady ourselves, falling back into known patterns.

Exercises

Listening Practice

When things are tough, it's really hard to hear the other person. Especially if you wish that they were saying something different. Something we learned early in our relationship, that has seen us through some difficult patches, and we now invite other couples to do in our workshops, is a powerful exercise called 'Listening Practice'.

This listening exercise sounds simple but is surprisingly effective. It can be uncomfortable to listen openly to your partner speaking, especially if we do not like or agree with what they are saying. And it is often uneasy to hold back our automatic reactions. It is difficult to actively remember what was said and reflect back accurately. You will find this exercise will help you to separate from your native reactions and warm the field between you, creating a safe space to speak and be heard. It is a practice to learn the skills of remaining available, receptive and aware, through partners taking turns in talking, listening and then reflecting back what they heard.

1. Designate an object to be used in this exercise. A stone, a mug, a tangerine, something that is comfortable to be held in the hand. Whoever holds this object is the designated listener.

2. Decide how long you want the listening practice to be. We recommend five minutes as a good time to start with.

3. Orient yourselves sitting opposite each other in good light with a soft, relaxed open body posture.

4. Decide who goes first. That person takes the 'listening object' and listens for five minutes. The other person then speaks about themselves and makes 'I' statements, such as 'I feel . . .' or 'I think . . .'

5. The listener cannot interrupt. They should also refrain from making any signals, other than to show they are listening.

6. When five minutes is up, the listener mirrors back what was heard as accurately as possible, using the same words the partner used as much as possible. If there are errors or things missed, the talking partner fills in the gaps. This mirroring can start with: 'I heard you say . . . is that right?' The listening partner is carefully checking to ensure they remember correctly.

7. Now swap roles.

NB: The partner going second should not use their time to make an argument or response to what their partner said in the first round.

When this exercise goes well, communication skills are built that can be used in everyday dialogue. One of the things that can prevent it from flowing is when the listener interrupts by responding verbally or nonverbally. If the listener finds it difficult to mirror back, the speaker can prompt them without criticism. It can help to have the attitude that they are doing their best. If there are important pieces of information that they don't seem to be able to mirror back, it can help to slow down as it could be content that is triggering for them.

4

Boundaries

What are boundaries?

Boundaries define your needs, expectations, desires and values for yourself, and in relationship to another person. Boundaries indicate to the other person what you are comfortable with, how you would like them to speak and behave towards you, and what you want to keep private and not share with them. A boundary marks the limits of an area, a dividing line, a border, a frontier. They show where one thing ends and another begins.

Having clear personal boundaries means you take responsibility for your own actions and emotions – yours and not other people's. Clear boundaries enable you to protect and respect yourself and to let others know what you need, so that you can remain connected to them – 'I don't want to be on this group text thread, so I'll leave now and look forward to seeing you all at the party.' Clear boundaries indicate that we can meet our own needs, that we aren't overly dependent on others to meet our needs, and that we have healthy self-esteem – 'I like going out with you, but I am not ready to start a sexual relationship just yet.' One way to improve self-esteem is to practise establishing clear boundaries. Clear boundaries are healthy boundaries.

There are two kinds of boundaries that are generated by the individual: internal and external boundaries. Internal boundaries (or implicit boundaries) are promises we make to ourselves, where we draw our own lines and make our own demarcations around what's OK and what's not OK. These might be boundaries around the way you want to live, what you eat, when you sleep, the use of your mobile phone, what you watch and read, and how you spend your time. The internal boundary also regulates the level of closeness and separation in the relationship, as we discuss further below.

The external, or explicit, boundaries are those we set with others, how we delineate our public contract and spoken agreements. When you take responsibility for your own actions and don't blame others, it means that you can try to stop worrying about the things that your partner, friends or family do that bother you. You draw your attention back to yourself, focus on your own sensation and feelings. You don't get caught up in other people's dramas and you don't let people take advantage of you. Of course, all this is easier said than done, it takes practice. When we get proficient at honouring our internal boundaries, the external ones become easier to manage too.

In addition to our individual boundaries, a couple also creates a boundary around itself. Boundaries can have physical and emotional limits: we might place boundaries around situations involving the home, leisure time, our private conversations and the level of intimacy we are comfortable with each other. We also create boundaries around what is OK to do outside the boundaries of the couple. Many couples might decide to be entirely monogamous. Some may like a sense of openness in their relationship and welcome flirting. Others might commit to ethical non-monogamy or polyamory. Once agreed, a boundary needs to be respected. If it's not respected, how much are we willing to take before calling it quits?

Both partners need to know how the relationship is defined. Boundaries and agreements make up the relationship container, which both supports the relationship and defines it. A relationship container needs to be strong enough to hold the relationship like a third skin. In the container, pressure can build, be held and tolerated so that change can occur. This container creates the individuals in the relationship, who in turn create the container. If there are holes in it – if boundaries and agreements are vague or not discussed – the relationship is weakened.

A strong container can hold the relationship together, especially in times of stress when it might be tempting to explore what's outside. This is often the time of crisis: when one partner has checked out emotionally, which often presents as restlessness or boredom, and is curious to look over the wall. Sometimes, the lid has already been opened and there has been a breach of the safety of the container. At other times, the container is locked so tightly that there is no room to breathe. How often do we hear people say they feel trapped in their relationship, like a prisoner? One partner can be a controlling force that another will want to run away from.

Managing closeness and separation in relationships

Boundaries allow you to set limits on how close someone can be with you. Regulating contact with others requires us to make, feel and state our boundaries. Clear boundaries create safety and security which help relationships thrive, as the more secure the container, the deeper the potential for intimacy. The measure of trust in a relationship is being able to lean on a boundary and know that it is secure.

Intimacy is allowing another person into your inner life, and the safer we feel with someone, the closer we are likely to allow them to get. With our internal boundaries, we implicitly regulate how much intimacy we can tolerate. This modifies the ways we have sex and the kinds of emotive, intimate or awkward topics they are willing to discuss. A boundary provides safety to work through difficult issues without fear of your partner making an exit. The ability to play and have fun is also determined by the internal boundary.

A relationship is a constant negotiation, usually completely unspoken, about the amount of aloneness and togetherness between the couple. Even during times of harmony, there is a natural desire for times of solitude. Some require more solitude than others – this balance between contact and withdrawal is individual and related to the balance between extroversion and introversion.

Boundaries help each person figure out where they end and the other begins. This is differentiation: 'This is me and that is you. We are two separate people, with different needs, different perspectives, different responses, values, outlooks, priorities, feelings, histories and places in the world. We may be holding hands and facing the same direction, but we do so from two distinct places. Distinct, individual beings, each with their private space, with space between us.'

However, when there is a lack of individual boundaries, where there is no real differentiation, we are taken into the arena of merging. Then, we are meshed, losing ourselves in another. At the beginning relationships usually start with a state of merging, where each partner feels sublimely at one with the other. Boundaries dissolve between you. You both make efforts to fit with each other in ways that retain the illusion of oneness. Two people become one, and develop an identity as a couple, rather than just separately. Merging gives us a feeling of security and safety: we have found someone to build a life with, a soulmate, a partner who we share ourselves with.

But then, as the relationship comes out of the honeymoon phase, there is a need for something new and a step needs to be taken so that each person can find their individual identity within the relationship, even if the other partner might not like it. However, this doesn't always happen and the couple may remain merged. People who are anxious and needy (like the 'octopus' we describe below) are likely to sacrifice their identity to receive the love and affection they crave.

Boundary styles: the octopus and the turtle

In the 1960s, psychologist John Bowlby coined the term 'attachment' to describe how we learn to manage closeness and separation in relationships. The three main styles he identified are anxious, avoidant and secure. (There is also a fourth style, known as disorganised attachment, which is a combination of the anxious and avoidant styles.) Some of us pursue and run towards our partner to regain connection when it is lost or threatened, and Bowlby referred to these people as 'anxious'. Others move away and withdraw from the partner to self-protect from the perceived loss of connection, which Bowlby called 'avoidant'.

We like the analogy of the octopus and the turtle for these two styles. With all those tentacles, the octopus seeks out and moves towards connection, while the turtle is self-sufficient and prone to retreating into its hard shell. The dolphin is the mediating third between the octopus and the turtle at the extremes. The dolphin is the secure one, who swims confidently and with presence between the two, able to seek out the connection when needed and tolerate aloneness when necessary. Bowlby referred to these people as 'secure'.

The turtle will often be very resourceful and independent, and likes to restore and recharge in solitude or solitary pursuits. They will see to their own needs, making themselves a sandwich when they want to. In contrast, the octopus will ask you what you want and rush to get it, or make you the sandwich before even asking if you want it. They'll be there at the door when you've been out and want to know how you are doing and ask lots of questions. They're great at working the party.

Problems begin when the turtle and the octopus get together. Both of these creatures hold a secret that they are somewhat nervous about relationships, but, predictably, they manage their anxiety in opposite ways. The octopus seeks reassurance that they are loved by reaching out and pulling the turtle close; the turtle finds this rather alarming and pulls back into its shell. When this happens, the octopus gets more anxious and doubles down on its efforts to bring the turtle close. But by now, the turtle has turned and is slowly lumbering off to get out of the way. The octopus begins to feel scared and lonely and imagines abandonment. In desperation, the octopus gets angry and critical, trying to prise the turtle out of its shell with its tentacles. But all to no avail, as the turtle retreats further in an attempt to find the peace and solitude they need. In psychoanalysis, this pattern is called the core complex: the fear of abandonment on the one hand and the fear of engulfment on the other. The turtle needs a lot of space and time to feel safe enough to talk about their feelings. They quickly feel intimidated in the presence of the impatient octopus.

People with porous, weak or unclear boundaries can fall into one of two camps: they either take too much responsibility for the emotions and actions of others – the 'octopus' of attachment styles – or they expect others to take too much responsibility for their own emotions and actions – the 'turtle' of attachment styles. These two types of people often end up in relationships together, as it creates a compelling bond.

KIEREN AND SAM

Kieren and Sam are a young couple in their thirties who have been together for three years. Kieren would send short texts to Sam, keeping her updated with his day. He just thought it was nice to make a connection by telling her what was going on. Sam thought this was rather odd. She would be out with her friends and didn't need to know what he was doing. She described the feeling of just being engrossed in doing her own thing with her friends and not giving him much thought.

Kieren has to go to a work event and is away for a few days. One lunchtime, he has a brief chat with Sam, then later in the day sends her a text: 'Hey babe, can we speak later?' A text returns: 'Hi Kes, we've already spoken today. We'll talk tomorrow.' Kieren is a little hurt and worried.

Sam said she felt baffled by his need to speak and couldn't see why it was necessary. In her mind, she was not being unkind or cold, she simply didn't need the same level of contact as Kieren. She was more the turtle, getting on with her own thing in her world. Kieren was the octopus, asking for reassurance, reaching out and checking in. But Sam wasn't reading this as him making a bid for connection, she thought he was being a bit clingy. But really, he was asking the critical question: are you there for me? Are you present? Am I present to you when I am not there? That's where trust is necessary, that even when you aren't together, you want to know that the other is holding you in mind.

Throughout the day, partners will make subtle movements towards and away, opening and closing to each other. When our partner does or says things that annoy or hurt us, we close off for a moment or, at different times, for hours or days. When our partner delights and interests us, we move towards them with joy and openness, feeling connected and together. Presence is staying there, allowing the movements to ebb and flow without pulling you off balance.

Closing the exits

Getting things right at the beginning is important to set the stage for the smooth evolution of the relationship. Sometimes it is difficult for one person or both to renounce other romantic opportunities, which makes it hard to create a strong sense of identity as a couple. Some people like to retain a relationship from the past in some form or another. Such as holding onto the lingering sense of security with their ex-lovers; they cling to an idealised vision that they can continue being friends with them while they pursue a new romance.

WILLOW AND BRAD

Willow and Brad have been together for a few years. But Willow is uncomfortable that Brad goes off to see his ex-wives and children twice a week. It's a routine: Sunday afternoon he visits and stays overnight with Cynthia and Wednesday afternoon he visits and stay overnight with Natalie. Nothing is going on sexually or romantically with his exes. Brad just wants to stay close to his children. It's difficult for Willow because she doesn't feel the number one priority in his life. Adding to the problem is the fact that when Willow wants to go out with her friends, she senses Brad getting grumpy with her. The truth is Brad is keeping his connections open with his ex-wives because he has an octopus attachment style. He came from a big family and loves the sense of being in the middle of all the action. He wants to hold everyone close to soak up the love; he can't get enough of it. When Willow goes out with her friends, Brad tells himself he's missing out and feelings of anxiety flood his body. Neither of them feel secure in the relationship even though each of them is committed to making it work.

One of the requirements for creating a strong boundary is to 'close the exits', or shut the door on other opportunities and adventures, in whatever form this might take for you. In a monogamous relationship, this would include making the choice to only sleep with your partner; in a polyamorous relationship, it might look like committing to your partner romantically and sexually as your primary partner, but choosing to have casual sex only with others; or perhaps it might look like pursuing sex together as a couple, but never independently. Whatever works for you both, making a commitment is a prerequisite for the emergence of the third body between you.

How to create boundaries in a relationship

Where are the boundaries of the relationship? Boundaries are where you decide they are. Some people have clear boundaries that are non-porous and impenetrable. Others have permeable boundaries that are leaky or perhaps even non-existent. Often boundaries exist around individuals and couples without much awareness or communication between the couple about their importance.

Negotiating boundary agreements

Within the limit of most intimate relationships, there are specific thresholds agreed upon by the couple. How do we know where these are? Sometimes these are stated but more often they are only discovered by crossing them. A marriage ceremony is a ritualistic announcement of a commitment to a boundary; the couple standing at the foot of the aisle are announcing 'we are together!'. It heralds a dividing line to the rest of the world – 'this is us; that is you'. The commitment creates a partition, a natural exclusivity, which is necessary for the couple to thrive.

The definition of monogamy used to be that we only have one partner in our lifetime. Now it means we have a sexual relationship with only one partner at a time. When a couple is choosing monogamy as their preferred style of relationship, the boundaries may be defined in some ways – i.e. a couple commit to one another emotionally and sexually – so for many monogamous couples who commit to each other, the boundaries may be similar to those of a marriage. Whether married or not, most couples will define themselves as exclusive in some way or another, whether this is emotional or sexual. All boundaries are different.

Of course, there are many other ways in which to flourish in intimate relationships, but the boundaries in these may be less obviously clear and might take more active discussion to establish. For example, ethical non-monogamy, including polyamory, is having intimate relationships with multiple people at the same time. In other words, you can have more than one romantic partner. Ethical non-monogamy is based on agreement, consensus and trust, where a couple will inform each other about their intentions and get consent before having sex with anyone else. This may also include inviting other people to join them in a group of three or more. Even in the most open relationships, there are certain boundary agreements that are essential for creating a safe, relaxing container. For example, it is normal and healthy to find other people attractive outside the relationship. But the feelings of the individual and between you as a couple – for instance, how robust you are emotionally in yourself and in the relationship – will determine whether flirting by your partner is deemed hurtful or a threat. This might be the case in some open relationships, too – it depends upon your individual boundaries as a couple: everyone is different.

Within any relationship, each person has their own sense of where the line is drawn. Sometimes this is in the same place as our partner; sometimes it's wildly different. Some like a sense of openness in their relationship and welcome flirting, while their partner may experience their partner's flirting as a betrayal. For some couples, having sex with others is OK; for other couples, it's very much *not* OK. Having many children or none at all and leaving the washing up till tomorrow or not – these represent boundaries too.

But many people do not talk about where their boundaries are; they are tacit expectations, only discovered when a boundary is transgressed. Often couples expect the other to have the same boundaries and then find out they don't. But it is rare in a couple for each individual to consider the boundaries to all be in the same place, so they need to be negotiated and agreed between you. One partner may want clear boundaries, while the other prefers them to be more relaxed. Boundaries that are too loose or undefined can cause a sense of insecurity in the relationship, but if they are too tight, they can cause suffocation. Different expectations of boundaries can easily cause hurt and conflict in a relationship.

It is necessary for each partner to feel comfortable with the agreed form of the relationship internally, in themselves, and to know that both of them gain from the clarity. No one wins if one of you is agreeing to something because you feel there is a compulsion to do so. Once agreed, a boundary needs to be respected and, if needed, renegotiated. Over time, boundaries can move for each individual too, so it's a complex area that can take some delicate navigation. It can be difficult for partners when one of you wants to redefine a previously agreed boundary in the relationship. Not all relationships survive this, but some do.

Hurt or rupture is inevitable at times and these instances are often repaired through a compassionate discussion and the making of a new agreement. But often a serious and unequivocal boundary violation can occur when one partner has an affair, which can be either emotional or sexual. Not all relationships can recover from an affair, but many do. In these instances, the boundaries can be repaired and rebuilt over time, potentially deepening the connection between you. We look more at affairs in the following chapter.

Happy couples allow the discussion about boundaries to be open and ongoing. In a healthy, happy relationship, boundaries are more likely to be fluid, yielding, circumstantial, unpredictable and often contradictory. But the couples are aware that the boundaries are there and they can talk about them. It can be helpful to think of boundaries as existing along a continuum: while some are fixed and non-negotiable, others are more fluid. Perhaps we prioritise kindness, respectful dialogue and spending time with our partner. Then there will be other issues we are more flexible around. These may still be things you have decided are important, but instead of feeling like rules, or deal breakers, these boundaries may be more like guidelines. As long as you are both in agreement, flexible boundaries are healthy. When you are agile together, you leave room for each of you to grow.

STEVE AND LOTTIE

Steve wanted to redefine his monogamous marriage into a polyamorous relationship. His wife Lottie was dead against it. There were no easy answers; they had been experiencing severe conflict for a while in many parts of their relationship. Steve's fear of owning and talking about his bisexuality with Lottie was aggravated by Lottie shutting him down every time he brought it up, leaving him feeling lonely and isolated. Their relationship had come to an impasse, which prompted Steve to divulge his motivations and desires.

When Lottie could confront her fear of losing him, she realised that in shutting him down she had lost him already. By accepting his desires, she regained the part of him that had been split off. Steve realised it was his internalised shame that had held him back from talking to Lottie. As he began to talk about his sexuality, he could then begin to risk being himself with her and gain the acceptance he longed for, not only from her but also from himself.

This new level of vulnerability was exhilarating for them both and gave their relationship and each of them individually the vivacity and sparkle they had been lacking. Their intimacy deepened not only with each other but also with themselves. They began to make other choices and decisions that had previously been closed off to them as they became more adept at communicating their fears and fantasies. Lottie became better at knowing what she needed to feel reassured and found ways to communicate that to Steve. They decided to experiment by going to swinging clubs together. This felt less threatening to Lottie, as she could still feel in connection with Steve, and it satisfied Steve's wish to open the relationship. They managed the potential anxiety of this by taking time to get support from their friends and reassurance from each other.

Knowing what we want and don't want

Getting together with another person is stepping forward with a big bold 'yes'. It takes bravery to confirm a 'yes' with conviction and assertiveness, it takes courage to commit. *Yes* I want to be with you; *yes* I love you; *yes* you are the one for me.

Saying 'yes' helps us to feel connected, close, together, unified, part of a team. But if we can't say no, then the yes can't be trusted. The yes is only potent when it is given freely, as freely as a no would be given. Saying yes or no is making a commitment. It is making a boundary between one thing and another. This or that. You or me or the relationship.

Saying yes to something is classifying it. It classifies it as important to you, as worth having. Saying yes is making a boundary to include the yes and exclude the no. You can't have both.

Can you say 'no'?

Many people are conflict averse. They veer away from it; they hate rejecting and being rejected and will do anything to avoid it. They prefer to say yes to someone else at the expense of saying no to themselves. An inner voice is saying 'no!' but fear of hurting someone, or not being liked by them, or creating a fuss, or upsetting the status quo, or going against the flow, or of feeling selfish or guilty will have them saying 'yes' instead. There can also be a discomfort in hearing 'no' – it can trigger childlike feelings of rejection in us, which put us back in that vulnerable place. It is likely that when someone who is conflict averse heard a 'no' as a child and they weren't getting their needs met, they then told themselves their needs didn't matter.

Many of us have been socialised to avoid saying no. We have been taught to fit in, go along with things and adapt ourselves to other people's wishes. These are the marks of 'people pleasing'. If this is you, practise saying no, even though it may trigger insecurities and may mean tolerating the risk of being disliked or losing approval.

If you are someone who often over-extends your capacity by agreeing to things, it may be because you find it hard to say no. You may also find it hard to set boundaries on your time and to prioritise your own agenda. It can help to acknowledge the pain that it may impact the other – 'I realise this isn't the answer you were hoping to get . . .' – and to help them connect with the need behind their request. If it isn't an absolute 'no', offering an alternative is also helpful – 'How about tomorrow instead of tonight?' 'What about going to the cinema instead?' 'What would you like as an alternative?'. If you say no to your partner, with or without other suggestions, do they take it as a major rejection? Do they then get angry or grumpy, or withdraw? It is common for couples to get into a habitual cycle around rebuffs and rejections as they bring up lots of emotions.

When one person is making a request and the other is saying no, it creates an oppositional stance. How this is managed says a lot about the relationship. If one partner's 'no' triggers painful feelings from the past, how can the couple navigate this? If the pattern is to react defensively or to withdraw, what would it take to stay in level contact? Often a 'no' can be heard as carrying an underlying message that we are not good enough, too little or too much, so how can we self-soothe to manage that feeling and stay in the present with our partner?

How do we know a 'yes' from a 'no'? Sometimes it's so clear we're without a doubt but other times, without necessarily being aware of it, we'll have a gut feeling, an instinct, a hunch. We get a felt sense of a reaction and we act on it. That felt sense is called interoception, your brain's perception of the signals of the body's state. It can be felt like a temperature reading of our own heartbeat or internal organs, tension in the muscles, a dialogue between heart and brain or digestion and brain. Interception allows us to 'tune in' to our body responses and read those signals. We don't necessarily diagnose which message we are responding to but, overall, it arrives with us as a gut feeling, an instinct or a hunch, which leads us to say a 'yes' or a 'no'. Depending on our emotional state, we will read these signals slightly differently. People who are depressed report a reduced ability to feel bodily signals, so for them the 'instinct' may be much quieter. While people with anxiety may interpret a small change in heart rate as being much bigger than it really is, which can amplify the sense of stress.

Having the embodied knowledge of authentic choice helps us to distinguish the flavour of our responses. This is essentially our gut response: for some of us it is clear, we feel it as an intrinsic knowing. At other times this embodied knowledge is elusive, a guess based on uneasy feeling or a hunch. It can take practice, especially when if we have been socialised to say yes and go along with things as they are, or go along with other people's desires.

JACKSON AND AVA

Something that Jackson and Ava find difficult in their relationship is an imbalance in how they make requests of each other. Jackson doesn't ask Ava for anything, doesn't make requests or even invitations. Ava, on the other hand, feels that she continually asks Jackson to do things, to listen to her, cuddle her and go on dates with her. Over time, she feels the lack of requests from Jackson as a rejection. He won't even ask her to pass the salt on the table or to make him a cup of tea. It's not that he doesn't like being cared for but he would like her to know what he wants and just get it for him. Ava tries her best but it's a guessing game that she finds tiring and unsatisfying. Jackson ends up disappointed that he doesn't get what he wants, but still he finds it impossible to ask.

Jackson is reacting to unconscious memories of his mother who was not able to provide for him or give him attention. As a child, his requests were repeatedly turned down by an overworked and distracted matriarch. Every time he heard 'no' it wasn't only about the thing he wanted, it was about the connection to love, care and attention he yearned for. He learned that if he doesn't ask, he won't get a 'no', which would be devastating for him to hear. If you can't tolerate hearing a 'no', it's unlikely you will ask for anything.

Ava feels this as a distancing and it bothers her; she wants to feel him there. She wants to know his preferences, his choices; she wants him to reach out to her, to ask her and invite her. She wants to feel wanted. This detachment activates something familiar for her as she didn't feel particularly valued or wanted in her family of origin. Their wounds match.

Jackson learns that his independence is really anti-dependent and anti-relational. He begins to see that he is holding himself out of the relationship and avoiding intimacy with Ava, which is hurtful to her. Ava sees that the pressure she puts on Jackson to ask her for things is also keeping him away because he fears the trap of dependence. Ava holds off from encouraging Jackson to ask and he starts to feel it is safe to come towards her with a few simple requests.

Because of the infrequency of his requests, Ava had felt it impossible to decline whatever it was he asked for, and if she did decline, it seemed to devastate Jackson. This put her under a lot of pressure to 'go along with' Jackson's rare requests, even if she wasn't very willing. She learns that when she is in her own truth and free to say yes or no, this is a gift – she is saying more about who she is. She learns to be clear and to allow Jackson to tolerate her answer in his way, even if he is upset at first.

Jackson also learns not to fear hearing a 'no' from Ava. This happens when he understands that he can say 'no' to her and that it is also OK for her to do the same. Starting with simple awareness and practice, Jackson and Ava learn how to develop healthy interdependence for a more intimate relationship.

Can you say 'yes'?

We may not always know how to check in with our own inner compass of what feels right for us. Many of us are so cut off from our feelings, we smother them, deny them, run from them. We might be so disconnected from ourselves and our desires that we have no idea of what we feel about something.

Relationships begin with yeses. Maybe you remember your first 'yes' with your partner as you began to get to know each other – 'Yes, I'm interested in you.' 'Yes, I'd like to go out with you.' 'Yes, I want to kiss you.' 'Yes' is the receptive state; it opens doors and builds bridges. Throughout a relationship, continual yeses help to build commitment and confirmation. 'Yes' creates connection and constructs the essential 'third body' that lives in the space between you.

Many of us are quite ambiguous in our communication styles: we answer 'OK, if you want', 'all right'. There's not a right or wrong but it can be really helpful to be clear. Rather than answering to please someone else, check in with a gut sense or intuition – what does your hunch say and is it possible to be clearer? Of course, this is important in sex. We want our partner to have an enthusiastic 'yes!' all of the time. Anything short of that simply isn't consent.

But saying yes, affirming and including, automatically creates a 'no' from what is excluded, what is not this, not here or not going to happen. When we move towards one thing, we move away from another. A 'yes' to one thing is a 'no' to something else. Knowing where our 'yes' and 'no' lie can help us to know our own edges, our own boundaries. Where do you begin and end? What are your issues, wants, desires, and what are your partner's? It's important to respect your partner's boundaries, their specific yeses and nos.

'Yes' and 'no' are binary. You either want it or you don't. You either stay or go. You love them or you love them not. Yet, life isn't usually so straightforward. Our responses are not always so direct. Between the 'yes' or 'no' is a third way – a maybe, a probably, a 'willing to try it', a 'I don't know for sure but I might be interested'. In these days of heightened awareness around consent, we have learned that 'no means no' and 'if it's not a clear yes, it's a no'. We agree with that. Yet, is there room, in the safety of an intimate loving relationship, for yeses and nos to be fluid? Can we be contrary and contradictory sometimes? We said 'no' last week but 'yes' this week. We said 'yes' to it yesterday but we say 'no' to it today. We might like it if it was a bit different or perhaps we'll consider ending it in the middle after all. This could apply to anything: it might be sex, a date, a conversation – anything. The challenge we are proposing to you is to practise variety. If you're well practised in clarity, can you tolerate fluidity? And the inverse: if you're very familiar with your 'maybe', can you tolerate being decisive? In a relationship, this adaptability means we can meet our partner anew, respecting this person for the mysterious, divine being that they are.

In our workshops, one of the exercises we offer our participants is to feel the embodied sense of being acknowledged with a 'yes'. Partners stand in front of each other. One takes some steps backwards and grounds themselves by planting their feet on the floor and noticing their breath. Then they take a step forward, saying out loud the words, 'I am here.' The other partner receives them with 'Yes!' – an affirmative acknowledgement of their existence, that they are accepted and they belong. When the 'yes' is said with conviction and consistency, it confirms trustability – 'You can count on me.' 'You are important to me.' 'I am so very glad you are here.' We encourage them to repeat it, again getting some distance so they can have room to move forward towards their partner, but this time stepping forward with more energy: 'I Am Here!' The receiver then matches their energy with the oomph of their 'Yes!' to receive them. A third time, they actually leap forward, with a bit of a run-up – 'I AM HERE!' – and are met with gusto in voice and body: 'YES!'. It can touch a vulnerable place to dare to show up, announcing ourselves in our fullness, but it is equally exhilarating to be received and accepted in this way.

Taking risks and being vulnerable

We might fear that setting clearer boundaries will put our relationship in jeopardy, that saying what we need or want might risk our connection. It is possible that it will. It might risk losing it or, alternatively, it might deepen the intimacy. Without clear boundaries, we are not giving our all to our partner. We're holding back, offering them a mask, a veneer, a nice presentable facade, but not the real thing. When others trespass on our space, it is an act of kindness to be direct and clarify your position, both for them and you.

Clear boundaries feel risky but this is also why they are sexy: they differentiate us from our partner, they establish a space between two people which can create a frisson, an aliveness. This is something we say more about in a later chapter. When somebody states their boundary, we know where they are. They allow us to see them in all the vulnerability that it takes to show up and state 'here I am'.

DEAN AND THEO

Dean and Theo have been together for two years. Theo moved in with Dean a few months ago and was surprised to find that Dean still kept a box of his ex-girlfriend's stuff under the bed. Dean was annoyed at Theo's request that she come and pick it up. He resented Theo for asking this. Dean felt it was a curb on his freedom, curtailing his relationship with his ex. He liked the feeling of still having a connection with her. But Theo was worried in case Dean still felt a sexual attraction to his ex-girlfriend. Dean had always kept in contact with his exes and didn't think his bisexuality was a threat to his relationship with Theo, as none of his other partners had found this a problem. Despite Theo's worries, Dean resolutely refused to make a firm boundary and close things off with his ex, thinking it was against his nature. Dean liked to keep things fluid, just like he was in his sexuality. He didn't see he was doing any harm whatsoever and couldn't understand why Theo was so uptight. Later, it began to dawn on Dean that this was impacting his relationship with Theo, who was distant and less engaged than before he moved in. Dean realised that keeping his ex's stuff was a way of protecting himself from the risk of committing to Theo by investing in an exclusive relationship. He liked having his options open. Dean also came from a big family where they all stayed close and connected and he was unconsciously creating a sense of 'family' around him with his ex-partners.

Theo and Dean started a process of talking and healing. Theo told Dean how he was looking for security and needed to know that he was really wanted by Dean. Theo said how he had never been sexually interested in women, so couldn't help feeling nervous about Dean 'swinging both ways'. He said he was scared Dean might decide he wanted to date a woman again and leave him. Dean understood Theo's concerns and expressed how he was totally committed to Theo. He realised that he didn't want to leave Theo but neither did he want to lose the part of himself that liked women. He wanted to feel this part was acknowledged and accepted by Theo, not denied and ignored as it had been. Without this acceptance, he could not feel he could bring all of himself to the relationship with Theo. Dean needed to honour the authenticity of his bisexuality. Although this was challenging for Theo, he realised that he had freely chosen to date Dean knowing this about him. Importantly, after digging deeper, Theo acknowledged that he found these aspects of Dean exciting and erotic.

After these honest disclosures, their relationship deepened and felt more secure to both of them. A few *months later, Dean realised his ex-girlfriend's stuff had lost its emotional meaning for him. The box had become clutter and was now superfluous.*

Our story

How 'contactable' are you? How can I reach you? These are questions we asked each other as we sought a joint resolution around mobile phone use.

It might seem innocuous, even trivial, yet our different expectations around these boundaries has caused much anguish over the years. When we got together, mobile phones weren't in common use; as they became ubiquitous, it took some negotiation to find a way that worked for us both. We expected the other to have the same needs around contact during the day, but we don't. Discovering these false assumptions has been revelatory.

Sarah turned off her phone at work and sometimes didn't think to turn it back on. When Matt tried to reach Sarah and couldn't get through, he would quickly slip into annoyance, telling himself that Sarah didn't care about him – she was just in her own world, not considering his needs, not having him in mind. When Sarah would eventually turn her phone back, there would be missed calls from an anxious Matt reaching out. Sarah would return the call, thinking there must be some big drama or that an accident had happened, only to hear that the problem was that she hadn't been in contact.

What this revealed to us was our different needs around connection and engagement. For Sarah, with her tendencies to draw back into self-sufficiency, there was no need to stay in contact throughout the day. For Matt, with his tendencies to reach out and seek contact, he needed to know she was there for him.

Over time, we became more compassionate with each other's needs for space and connection, for reassurance and independence. Sarah learned to let Matt know when she would be offline and Matt learned to let Sarah know how much he appreciated feeling her there. Once we learned to understand each other more and have more trust in our bond, these issues dissipated. Sometimes nowadays, it also happens the other way around: when Sarah is away from home, she will call Matt for a chat and he's busy and doesn't need to talk.

Exercises

Yes/No/Maybe

This is an exercise for couples to explore the theme of boundaries. There are many ways of doing this exercise and touch is a way for couples to raise their awareness of sensate signals and their responses. We enjoy this exercise for the opportunity to practise being clear with ourselves and our partner, and the experience of expressing and tolerating a 'yes', 'no' 'or 'maybe' response.

- One person is the 'giver' and the other the 'receiver'.
- The receiver sits in a chair or lies down, whichever is most comfortable for them.
- The giver touches their partner in a variety of ways. Caressing, nuzzling, clasping, patting, stroking,

rubbing, with various tempo, pressure and parts of their body. They avoid genitals and chest and any other part that the receiver wants avoided.

- Their receiver gives feedback, limiting their response to either 'yes', 'no' or 'maybe' – adding in 'yes please' when things feel really good. They can't explain why or discuss it, at least not until the end of the exercise.

- The giver modulates their touch, to elicit each of the four responses – 'yes', 'no', 'maybe' and 'yes please'.

If the 'giver' continually hears 'no', and can't seem to touch their partner in a way that elicits a 'yes', stop the exercise and discuss it. Either the receiver has a low tolerance to being touched right now or the giver isn't finding creative ways to offer alternatives that might invoke pleasure.

When we love our partner, we want them to be happy and we want to please them. That can mean we veer towards only wanting 'yeses' and 'yes pleases'. Yet, if we veer away from anything that we're not sure about or might be risky, we limit our range of movements and eventually it will become boring, predictable and lifeless. We can kill the relationship if we can't risk discovering a 'no'. Often in this exercise, couples discover new ways of touching their partner that they had no idea they would enjoy. This exercise helps us find out where our boundaries are; sometimes we find them by crossing them or by bumping right up to them.

5

Transgressing Boundaries

Relationships need the form or structure of boundaries and agreements to contain them. But the structure is only half the story. How couples conduct themselves within the structure that they have chosen is crucial. Can they communicate and be honest with their feelings? Can they be respectful and ask for what they want or will they be manipulative and play games? Will they validate each other's needs and respect boundaries? Or will they be coercive to get their way and dismiss and discount others? Can they take responsibility for their own choices and feelings, without blaming or taking out their anxiety and anger on others? A satisfying relationship demands that we conduct ourselves in an honest, open, loving and compassionate way. But even if one partner betrays the other, healing and repair is always possible.

Betrayals and affairs

What is betrayal and what is an affair? Do secret sexual or intimate online relationships constitute an affair when they involve neither intercourse, oral sex, nor any kind of actual physical contact? The answer is yes because of what these kinds of relationships invite. An emotional affair is where you start engaging with another person in a way that invites sexual frisson and even the promise of sexual contact. This could be a liaison at work which morphs into something more intimate. Perhaps you start sharing personal stories, contacting them out of office hours and then begin chatting with them for hours in secret, ignoring the pain this may be causing your partner. Whatever it is that is going on, whether or not the behaviour is considered acceptable will be determined by the sense that we have indeed crossed a boundary. Everyone who has been betrayed will have no doubt when a line has been crossed.

Betrayals as a breach of trust

In a relationship, betrayals happen when a prior implicit or explicit agreement is contravened or when a known boundary is transgressed. As we saw in the previous chapter, most partners don't consciously set out the parameters of what they want, what they expect and what they absolutely won't tolerate. It is often worked out by trial and error as they go along. The relationship container is often shaped by negative and positive feedback and behavioural adjustments on the hoof, not always by prior agreement. When boundary transgressions are made unknowingly, this is not always experienced as a betrayal. A betrayal, such as an affair, on the other hand, is felt as a clear boundary transgression. When a betrayal happens in any kind of relationship, it is the breach of trust that feels most difficult to manage for the betrayed partner. Betrayal is felt in the body as a painful bodily sensation.

The most difficult aspect of betrayal is the loss of the coherent sense of reality that has been shattered. The trusted past, the ground upon which you have built your present experience, now becomes questionable and full of doubt. There is also the self-recrimination, the horror of having been fooled and duped into believing falsehoods. When someone finds out they have been betrayed, they want to regain their sense of order. They want to know what was real and what wasn't. When did the betrayal take place? What happened on that occasion when your partner was supposedly working late? Was that an excuse? That lovely beach holiday you had, was that all a sham?

Defining the meaning of affair

Affairs are a particular kind of betrayal and as old as the hills. For the person having the affair, the taboo makes them exciting and the secrecy adds to the allure. Marriage and long-term relationships can get boring. The same person, the same arguments, the same social circle, the same dishes. A relationship, whether or not it is monogamous, is built on trust. Infidelities and affairs involve disloyalty or unfaithfulness to a partner in what was supposed to be an exclusive relationship. Affairs are very common; a survey revealed that 60 per cent took part in them yet 90 per cent of people disapprove of them. Their marginalisation is part of their attraction. They live in the shadows, hidden and often steeped in shame.

Emotional affairs, which do not include sexual contact, are also a type of affair – an affair of the heart, still an infidelity. Although the dynamics are similar, the lack of an overtly sexual component does not mean that the volatility and sense of betrayal is any less: keeping any important aspect of yourself hidden is a betrayal. Keeping secret bank accounts, gambling and other kinds of addictions that are kept hidden, and any kind of lie are duplicitous. The most threatening aspect is not the behaviour itself but the dishonesty that it casts over the entire relationship.

Flirting can also be experienced as a betrayal in some cases. Flirting can be fun and not dangerous unless one person in the relationship is constantly flirting with the same or similar people and is using it as a way to exit the relationship. It's normal to be attracted to other people but when we are in a relationship that excludes extra parties to the couple and we pursue that attraction in secret, we're breaking a boundary.

Self-betrayal

How do we know when we have betrayed our partner? Any betrayal of another person begins with a betrayal of the self. We betray ourselves the moment we choose to renege on a commitment we have made to ourselves, when we have an affair while we are married, in a monogamous relationship or when we go outside of any of the agreed limits in an open relationship. When we have transgressed a boundary in the relationship we will know it somewhere in ourselves: the pang of a guilty conscience combined with the excitement at the prospect of the shiny new thing. Self-betrayal is ignoring the inner voice of conscience. It is losing sight of our own inner wisdom, our wishes, hopes and dreams, and not operating from the centre of our being.

We know about self-betrayal from the countless other ways we go back on commitments we make to ourselves, such as breaking a promise we made to ourselves, letting our dreams go unheeded or giving up on things we said were important to us. Making a commitment to a friend and then not turning up is a betrayal to yourself as well as to your friend. Every time you give your word to yourself or another and then don't stand behind it, this is a self-betrayal.

We also betray ourselves every time we don't stand up for what we need because we feel too ashamed, too timid or shy, or just think that we're being silly. We may seek a way to repair our self-betrayals by vowing not to do the same things again. Perhaps we have been hurt and betrayed by another and we vow to ourselves that we will never get into that situation again, such as an abusive relationship, or when we have been losing ourselves in addictive behaviours.

Why do people have affairs?

There are many reasons that people end up having affairs. These can include feeling neglect and indifference from our partner; feelings of deadness, despair, loneliness; sexual frustration; the search for emotional support and affection, as well as the variety of crises and conflicts that strain relationships and that couples might find easier to avoid instead. Contrary to common belief, many people who have affairs report being in happy marriages. They love their partner very much but they still have an affair to enhance their experience of life. But whether or not they see their relationship as happy, when someone has an affair, at least one partner in the relationship is not getting what they need from it and they look outside to get those needs met. Often it is assumed that this is sex, but it is more often something that is missing from the relationship itself, which might also include eroticism. As has been said: 'My relationship wasn't starved of sex, it was starved of a relationship.'

Although affairs can bring pain, hurt and grief to the betrayed partner, there is also the offer of expansion and self-discovery for the betraying partner. It's a self-centred strategy. Whatever the reasons, when someone has an affair, they feel valued, significant, and important to their lover; they feel needed. They think about each other all the time. They're tuned in, turned on, on the same wavelength.

Longing for the lost parts of oneself

People are often drawn into affairs because they seek in the affair partner parts of themselves they can no longer access because they have allowed them to wither away. This makes a strong attractive pull. They want those qualities that they see so vibrant and shining in the other, but don't realise that they are projecting lost aspects of themselves.

Relationships can lead people into compromising themselves too much to accommodate the other and over years of self-neglect, this can lead to frustration and dullness in the individual. They end up resenting the person they have become. It's not what the relationship has done to them, it's what they have done to themselves in allowing too much merging and not differentiating enough. They end up feeling like a 'nobody', disconnected from a felt sense of their bodily selves, bored and boring. Looking outside the relationship for excitement and validation helps them to feel attractive and potent again, and to reclaim a sense of agency. In connecting with the affair partner they feel valued and interesting. This kind of affair is a self-betrayal. The person avoids the work of rekindling their own inner flame and searching for, reclaiming and reintegrating aspects of themselves they allowed to perish. But if this can be done, the labour of bringing these aspects of themselves back into the relationship and differentiating from the partner can begin.

The relationship is too safe

Merging kills desire. This is because the so-called 'happy marriage' is sometimes too safe and too close for the erotic charge to build up between the partners. For the charge to spark between you there needs to be a space across which it can strike. But you get used to the closeness and friendship, believing that this is what happens when relationships mature. So you settle for that, telling yourself you're quite content really. But one day, bang! You meet someone and feel a charge. You rediscover your long-lost ability to flirt and show your spicy side in the spaciousness of this new encounter. An affair starts. You love the tantalising joint unfolding of your erotic natures in tandem with your affair partner in the thrill of the unknown. You're both in it together. Doing those things with your partner at home seems unthinkable. It's far too risky. You can't even be sure your partner would like that kind of thing now. After all, they didn't complain about anything missing any more than you did. The justification has begun. The affair continues.

SUZY AND REX

Suzy is in her mid-sixties and has been married for 30 years to her husband Rex. The last of their children have not long left home. She experiences the grief of the 'empty nest'. Rex has recently retired and is enjoying his time cycling with friends and restoring old furniture. But for Suzy, death seems to stretch ahead of her. She works part-time as an interior designer. One day, she is presenting a scheme she has been working on at a large design agency in a city a few hundred miles away. In the front row is George, the CEO of the agency. Their eyes meet and Suzy feels a tingle up her spine. He is handsome and toned, and a similar age to Rex. The team all go for a drink after the meeting and George stays close to Suzy all evening, chatting and laughing with her. She gets back late. She tells Rex all about her experiences as she usually would, but she omits to tell him about George. Thinking about him and that evening gives her a thrill, a feeling of aliveness that she hadn't felt for a while.

As contact with him continues, it is not only the sense of being seen and admired that is exhilarating for her but also the excitement of being 'naughty' after so many years of being a good mother and a good wife. Taking risks in keeping this secret is a way of distancing herself from her husband, who she dearly loves but they have become merged, fused, in a cosy, comfortable routine that had suited her well. It is safe and sweet but has become boring. She does not want to stop the liaison with George and an affair ensues, giving her a sense of vitality that she has not felt in a long time. She even starts wearing clothes she hasn't worn for years; her hair is shinier and her skin glows. The sex is obviously doing good things for her. Yet she knows she has a good relationship with her Rex. For sure it needed spicing up, but this wasn't the way to do it, she knows that. The affair would devastate him and it is also a self-betrayal. She can't believe she could do such a thing and she feels horribly guilty.

Suzy faces a time of reckoning. She realises she was seeking self-renewal now that she is standing at the gateway of her maturity. She could admit that she was scared of the sense of an abyss that retirement presented and the affair with George enlivens her and distracts her from her fears. She enjoys a full, rich life; she thrives on challenges and the feeling of making a positive contribution to other people's lives. But it is new to her to let Rex know what she wants as she has been used to putting his needs first. She enters a phase that is very uncomfortable for her, of practising self-disclosure with Rex.

She decides to end the affair with George. She can see it has been valuable in her life to help her get perspective on her current situation. She doesn't know if Rex will forgive her or if her marriage will survive, but she is willing to take the risk of transparency. It also means she has to re-evaluate her self-image as a 'good wife'. She can see it is the only way for her to move on with integrity and gain the vitality in life she so craves. She finds a way to tell Rex, who is of course shocked and hurt. He is faced with the challenge of either leaving the relationship or reappraising his internal model of Suzy. He chooses the latter and comes to appreciate Suzy's bravery in facing him with the truth. He is grateful to her for choosing him again, knowing she could have decided otherwise.

Mystery and uncertainty have withered and died

Intimacy is difficult: it requires vulnerability to allow ourselves to be seen on a deeper level. If sex stops or is very scarce we can feel unloved, unwanted, rejected, abandoned, unlovable. Other people seem mysterious, exciting, forbidden. Secrecy and taboo can become so utterly alluring.

When partners are so close that they entangle and lose a sense of individuation, it can lead to feelings of being smothered or swallowed up by the other and a loss of identity ensues. The challenge of a relationship is to find a place of balanced connection between aloneness and togetherness or, in the extreme, between abandonment and engulfment. Finding this balance means keeping enough space between you to allow each of you to be different while being close enough to feel you are cherished and important to each other.

There are all sorts of motives for having an affair. One of them is to call your partner's attention back to you if you are feeling neglected. Or, feeling abandoned, you give up on the relationship and seek attention elsewhere. Another is an unconscious motive to disrupt the status quo and transform the relationship. Or you have allowed yourself to be engulfed by the other partner and lost your identity, and you seek to break out and find yourself again. Eroticism and sexual frisson require at least some distance and separation, to be able to see your partner as 'other' to you.

Part of the allure of the affair is that the affair partner is another person, 'other' to the relationship partner. They do not carry any of the accumulated history, issues or problems of the relationship. They are a blank slate upon which desire and erotic fantasy can be projected. Another part of the appeal is that it is forbidden. Jack Morin, in his book *The Erotic Mind*, sets out the erotic equation as follows: attraction + obstacles = excitement. In other words, Morin says that we need some obstruction to our attraction for eroticism and excitement to build. That's why affairs can be so enticing because there is erotic charge and excitement due to the deceitful nature of the activity. Neither partner is really 'available' and there has to be careful planning for the affair to remain secret. Eroticism thrives on secrets and taboos. Transgressing boundaries is exciting in itself. An affair is therefore set up to be exciting from the start. When the safety of a relationship becomes stiflingly comfortable and predictable to the point of boredom, there can be a pull to experience risk. It's the tension between security and adventure. We want both. That's why affairs are usually not divulged. The person seeking an affair wants both the security of their existing relationship and the excitement and risk of something new.

SINÉAD AND JEREMY

Sinéad and Jeremy have been married for 14 years and they have two children. Sinéad discovers that Jeremy has concealed his long-term affair with another woman with whom he has two other children. When Sinéad finds out, everything shatters; her trust in him and everything they have built is thrown into question. The implications are immense for her and the children she shares with Jeremy. She is not sure if anything can be put back together between them.

They had been struggling for many years preceding his affair. Their relationship was strained and each of them felt locked into their own difficulties. They were both completely overwhelmed. Neither was able to communicate their needs or to offer the other support.

Jeremy concealed his desperation before starting the affair as he was scared of Sinéad's reaction. She had been depressed, he didn't want to hurt her and he could not bear the thought of abandoning her. Once the affair had started, he didn't want her to know. He didn't think she was strong enough to bear the shock.

Sinéad and Jeremy then have a long process of coming to terms with their situation that involves not only managing their current emotions but also looking at their relationship history and also further back into their individual childhoods.

For Sinéad, expressing her rage, and having Jeremy witness it, is an essential part of this. She is furious with him, with his behaviour and secrecy, with the sense of being cheated on and how the betrayal has shattered her sense of their life together. She doesn't know what is true anymore. Sinéad uncovers her own distress, unhappiness and her low self-esteem. When she looks back on her life she sees she lost her freedom to develop her professional life when unplanned pregnancies led her to put her career on hold and focus on raising the family. She feels grief and anger at this situation – she loves being a mum, yet *she hadn't let herself acknowledge the impact this had on her career path.*

Jeremy explores his fears about their joint struggles at the low point of their partnership and how they intersected with his own personal problems from childhood, all of which he kept hidden and suppressed. A crisis in their finances meant he worked all hours to keep the family afloat. This left Sinéad alone to cope with their son's behavioural issues and Jeremy's intrusive mother, all of which compounded the stress they felt.

Neither Sinéad nor Jeremy were able to access, let alone acknowledge to each other, the depths of their own personal and shared despair, which they each responded to in different ways and which increased as the years passed. For Jeremy, the affair acted as a pressure-release valve from his own inner turmoil and the hopelessness of the relationship.

Sinéad and Jeremy manage to repair this boundary breech, to untangle from a conflicted situation and move into a more spacious, respectful relationship. In looking back, they both acknowledge and regret that neither of them had the capacity, nor were supported enough at that time, to do things differently. Sinéad and Jeremy explore the circumstances that entrapped them in a stifling relationship, resulting in both partners seeing themselves and each other in a different light.

For some people, an affair that results in other children may be unforgivable. Sinéad does feel deeply betrayed, yet she doesn't want to walk away completely. She thinks about the vulnerabilities and pain and realises they are familiar to her. Sinéad's mother was the result of an affair which the extended family had known about but nobody talked about. The situation of Jeremy's two other children is complex and tricky to navigate. The lies over many years take a lot to forgive.

Sinéad gradually embarks on a new career path and commits to regaining her lost independence. She realises she needs the liberation of more space in the relationship and decides to move out of the family house into a flat of her own. Jeremy learns to tolerate the distance from her by developing his relationship with himself and giving her the space she needs. They work on rebuilding trust together.

Is it possible to heal after an affair?

Research suggests that around 50 per cent of relationships recover from affairs and are rebuilt. An affair can be a catalyst for change and renewal in the relationship. Staying in a committed relationship, even after a betrayal, increases satisfaction in the longer term. The bulk of research that currently exists centres heterosexual couples. It shows that if you're a man and you cheat, you are more likely to stay married. About 60 per cent of men who have affairs stay in their existing union. Women who cheat are less likely to remain married, with approximately 40 per cent staying in the relationship. This points to a situation where women who choose infidelity have already made their mind up about the relationship. Studies show that when women reach this point in a difficult relationship, it's a sign that things are serious and often irreversible. Infidelity can sometimes be a bid for attention or a warning cry for help, but it can also signify a search to recover parts of a lost identity.

An affair does not have to be sexual. Or it may be sexual and yet not be considered an affair. It depends on the boundaries agreed by the couple. One couple agreed to have an open relationship where sex with others was considered reasonable. But one of the partners felt that kissing was too intimate and they didn't feel comfortable with it, so both agreed that while having sexual intercourse was OK, kissing was not and they would not engage in kissing with other partners. Unfortunately, the kissing prohibition was not kept, the betrayed partner could not forgive the breach of the agreed conditions and the relationship ended. In another couple, one partner admitted to getting emotionally involved in an affair and engaging in kissing but not genital sex.

In any type of affair recovery, there are important steps to be taken for the violation of trust to be repaired, but this is not a guaranteed outcome because it depends on the emotional state of the couple and the attitude of the betraying partner. We are indebted to Sue Johnson for her research in this area. First the burden of guilt needs to be accepted by the betraying partner. This might sound obvious but sometimes there can be an element of blame on the other partner. The pain inflicted on the hurt partner must be fully acknowledged and the betraying partner will need to be able to empathise with their partner's suffering. The betraying partner must show remorse, express regret at their wrongdoing and make a full, heartfelt, honest apology. Often this has to be repeated many times over an extended period of time.

The betraying partner needs to be open to hearing the pain and disappointment in their partner and show patience and willingness to answer their questions. Some betrayed partners want to know more details than others, but usually there is a lot of work required to help the hurt partner patch together their shattered sense of reality. Depending on the level and duration of deceit, this could mean going over many years of corrupted memories. There needs to be a coherent narrative to explain the circumstances around the infidelity and how it happened. This does not mean making an excuse for what happened but is necessary for the betraying partner to fully understand all the circumstances so they can begin to rebuild safety and predictability in their partner.

Finally, there needs to be full commitment to change in the betraying partner, an assurance that it will not happen again and confirmation that all contact with the affair partner has ceased. This has to be backed up by showing what measures have been taken to ensure that trust will not be betrayed again and what lessons have been learned. Strategies to improve and enrich the connection between partners in the relationship going forward are also essential. When the injured partner can find enough trust to reach out and receive comfort from the betraying partner, there can be the possibility of rebuilding safety through this connection. All of the exercises we provide in this book will support the healing and repair needed for the couple to survive and thrive after an affair or betrayal but often additional help is needed to process the hurt. Even then, recovery of the relationship is not guaranteed.

How to avoid an affair

Look again with renewed curiosity and passion

When wanting to rekindle passion in your relationship, think of the day when you first met this person and were full of curiosity and intrigue. Practise the art of looking without preconception. Hold back from judgement, attune to your senses, notice accurately what you perceive through touch, body sensations, feelings and thoughts. Seek to expand yourself ever more to include new information about your partner and try new activities together. Above all, be open to discovering new things about yourself to share with your partner so you can bring something else to the table.

See your partner as if you're meeting them for the first time. Acknowledge that parts of them are a mystery, and allow them to keep some parts of themselves separate. Accept that maintaining a relationship means balancing transparency and privacy and constantly working to neither betray yourself nor your partner. Growth in a relationship is about allowing new parts of ourselves to flourish and change continually with our partner.

Tend to your own needs

It is important to find ways to nourish yourself enough to feel that you can thrive as an independent person. If there are activities you gave up at the beginning of the relationship, consider starting them up again. See it as finding the lost parts of yourself. Tend to your own interests and preferences. Seek out the flavours of life that you enjoy. Take your own sense of adventure seriously. Connect to your playfulness again. This means being true to yourself and acknowledging that your needs may be different to your partner's. Meet those needs yourself; do not rely on your partner to meet them for you.

Re-introduce novelty and uncertainty

Bring in uncertainty and novelty so your relationship can feel as exciting as an affair. How can you introduce the unknown, mystery, edge, surprises? Stoke adventure. Breaking rules energises us, makes us feel alive and vibrant.

- Take them on a surprise date, unknown destination
- Take a day together of non-responsibility
- Blindfold them and lead them somewhere new

Look at the exercises below for more inspiration.

Our story

There have been occasions when we have come up to the boundary of our commitment. We have both had attractions to other people: some of these were big crushes, some were little flirtations, many were fleeting fantasies. On a few occasions, we've caused each other pain and heartache that left an imprint on our relationship. Through feeling awkwardness, incongruity and the discomfort of reaching the limits that we have agreed to hold to, we learned what the commitment was. The edge of our contract is an awkward place to be.

Attractions have happened when we think we might get our needs met outside the relationship. Or when we are angry with the other and not able to express it cleanly. When we're feeling unacknowledged, unappreciated, unloved, we are more likely to consider this other person as being a potential source of what we need right now, to revive our sense of aliveness.

We've leaned right into the edge of our boundary of what's OK to understand what's not OK. Through trial and error, we discovered we have had different ideas of where the boundary is, or should be, or could be. Staying open to these conversations has caused both our behaviour to change and the boundary to shift.

There's the fairytale: two people fall in love, only have eyes for each other and live happily ever after. We hold that fairytale, on the one hand, as some ideal that we've been taught to believe is possible. Yet, on the other hand, we know that to be a fully alive adult human, attractions to many people are normal and healthy and part of a vibrant life.

How can we feel secure being 'the One' when other 'ones' are attracting our partner? At these moments when we have hit the boundary, we've resolved it by spending time going over what happened, telling each other how it happened, acknowledging each other's hurt and helping each other to understand how it happened. Patience for the needs of the other to understand this rebuilds trust. Over time, we also came to feel more secure in ourselves.

Exercises

Dates

When life is stressful and full of a host of pressures, time together as a couple can slip down the list of priorities. Regaining lost parts of yourselves together is essential to keep the relationship vibrant. This list of suggestions might inspire you to schedule different types of dates together, which are appropriate for your stage of the relationship.

Go on a surprise date night/weekends/time away together: Schedule time – for example, half an hour every week, a long evening once a month and a long weekend a few times a year.

A half-hour date could be:

- Offer them a massage in a new way
- Take them out for a walk somewhere you've never been in your neighbourhood; kiss while you're out
- Do a taste test of new food
- Put some music on and dance together
- Make love somewhere new

A long evening out together could be:

- Take them on a surprise date, unknown destination Leave your phones at home to minimise distractions and to increase the adventure, the sense of the unknown

A weekend date could be:

- If you have kids who are safe and happy enough with friends or family, and who are old enough to be left with them, then leave them for the weekend and don't check up on them. Let them know you'll be offline, unreachable and back at the end of the weekend. Take a weekend of non-responsibility.
- Go away and leave your phones at home (if your personal circumstances allow you to do this).

Think of your partner: When deciding what to do, check in – who is this for? If you arrange a gig, who likes the music? Is it you? Or your partner? If it's you, then it's a date for you and you can ask your partner if they are willing to come with you, to do something for you (giving them the genuine option to say no). Do not pretend it is for them if they are not interested in the band as it will backfire – they will feel unseen, coerced into going on this date with you and pressurised to enjoy it and be grateful. We're conditioned and taught to 'go along with', so we try our best to do that, but a little bit of us dies away, is disappointed, is discounted and shrinks. If you are using your partner for their company, then don't take them. Go to the gig on your own, or with someone else.

Surprise each other: Take turns planning a surprise, something you haven't done together before and you don't know if your partner has done before. The aim of this is to stoke your own aliveness, reignite your passion for adventure, seek novelty and make your own relationship exciting and a bit edgy, perhaps a bit taboo and surprising, something unpredictable or risky. Bring in uncertainty and novelty so your relationship can feel as exciting as an affair, making you feel alive and vibrant. It could be something adventurous or perhaps breaks some rule, real or imagined, that you have between you.

Date night: While this is important, take care not to let this be the only time you engage with each other, the only way you make love or have time for each other. Not only will it get expensive but it'll take away the ordinary art of being special at home.

Expectations: It can be disappointing if it is your partner's turn to organise a date and they find it difficult or don't know where to take you. This can feel dissatisfying – don't they know what I like? Aren't they excited to treat me? Aren't they confident enough to take a risk? Am I so fragile or hostile that they worry about getting it wrong? Do I have to tell them what I like? The one organising the date can sometimes be nervous – it's a big thing to surprise your partner, especially if you are taking a risk and doing something they, or you, have never done before. Do they like it? Are they disappointed? It can feel like a big responsibility to arrange things for them without them knowing, especially if you are used to talking over details of plans with them. You might need to self-regulate. The person being taken on the date should keep an open mind, appreciating the effort and willingness to take a risk, even if it doesn't always pan out as planned.

What could go wrong?: You might find you create the dates that you want: you take them to the cinema because you love the cinema, but do they? Or you get a massage for the both of you, as that's what you'd really want. And that's OK, as long as you know it's not something they would really dislike.

What could go well?: You have fun! You have a sense of adventure, you take risks, you feel yourself again as you meet your partner. You bring back a sense of mystery into your relationship. You build memories, you prioritise time together, you create a sense of excitement – you inject magic into the relationship again.

Conflict and Repair

*'Out beyond ideas of wrongdoing and right-doing,
There is a field. I'll meet you there.'*
– RUMI

Conflict is a normal part of a relationship

Severe, extended disruption and conflict is the antithesis of what we want in a relationship. It breaks the charmed bliss state of harmony. The bond breaks, we get hurt. It can trigger feelings of trauma and isolation, often rooted in childhood. There is a sense of powerlessness, of not being seen or understood, leading to frustration and anger.

Every relationship will have its own set of problems. No relationship is problem-free. Understanding that conflict is part of being human can help us tolerate difficulties and, when we accept them, we can discover creative solutions and find the middle ground. Many of the conflicts that surface in modern relationships arise from a belief that once we 'arrive' in the relationship, it will be free of problems: quarrel-free, worry-free, enduring bliss and companionship. This utopian fantasy is totally unrealistic and unreachable.

This delusion makes our current reality inferior, unwanted and less enjoyable. Also, if we feel we ought to be in utopia and we're not, then we can look for someone to blame. We may blame ourselves, but we also project the problems onto our partner. There's a myth that the grass is greener, that we can find a new partner and chase utopia. What we probably all know (but perhaps would rather not think about) is that if we leave this relationship, we'll find similar or another set of problems in the next.

Some couples have conflict habitually, as an ingrained part of the relationship. In these cases, rather than being in need of repair, it is a flavour of the bond. A 'combative alliance' is when conflict is the glue of the relationship. The heat is turned up as a way of connecting, an ongoing struggle for power and control that is painful and wearing. Hot or cold, fighting can be a form of intimacy. It is bonding over our specific intricate drama. The one thing the couple does agree on, even subconsciously, is that they will fight. They have a high tolerance for conflict, and something about the escalation feels safer than how life would be without it. Although the relationship would be healthier and more sustainable without it, these patterns can be hard to break.

Other people are conflict averse. They go to great lengths to avoid confrontation and challenging conversations for fear of causing an upset. As the years wear on, this avoidance leads to fewer and fewer safe discussion areas. There are now so many conversations to avoid for fear of coming into conflict. So many taboo areas. Why do we do that? Because we love each other so much that we don't want to rock the boat or upset each other. We don't want to take a risk. This protection is a lovely sentiment and yet we shrink the arena of possibility. And when that happens, we tiptoe around each other, avoiding anything risky, and we end up bored. The intention of protecting a loving and caring relationship ends up killing it: death by boredom. Couples have nothing to say to each other and sit across the table at dinner with nothing to discuss. Don't let this happen in your relationship. It's a sure sign of laying the foundations of disaster.

The cycle of harmony, disruption and repair

When we understand that conflict is a normal part of a relationship, with practice and skill, we can swiftly move to repair and then regain harmony. This cycle of harmony, disruption and repair is a function of a healthy, growthful relationship. It is the building block of trust when partners resolve the disruption together and arrive back in a harmonious state, usually with greater confidence in the emotional intelligence of the relationship.

Harmony and disruption are polar opposites. We can be getting on well with our partner, but then something happens and one of us gets upset, and we swing into a disrupted state. Repairing helps us to regain the connected state of harmony. Repair is the ability to step out of 'I am right, you are wrong' thinking and move to a higher plane of seeing you and your partner's position with empathy and compassion.

Repair is essential, but the disruption must happen first and is therefore crucial. It is the disruption that creates the golden opportunities for restoration. Repair builds trust, and the relationship grows and strengthens. As is true in any polarity in life, it is impossible to occupy one end of the pole permanently.

Strong bonds in relationships form when each person is tuned to the other and therefore gives and receives positive attention. But it is impossible to be completely attuned to your partner all of the time. There are inevitable ruptures in the connection when one of you is unavailable to the other. Sometimes these ruptures are minor and no significant harm is done. At other times, if one of you is particularly seeking attention and care, the disconnection may be more hurtful. These connection losses may range from a callous remark or non-empathic response to complete abandonment.

Behaviour patterns in adult intimate relationships have their roots in early life. We unconsciously look for a similar model to the one we experienced in infancy. The primal model for all our later relationships is the archetype of the mother or primary carer/child relationship. American developmental psychologist Ed Tronick studied the relationship between infants and caretakers. He found that a harmonious relationship, which he called 'interactive synchrony', is attained when there is matching attunement and reciprocity between the caretaker and infant. The researchers micro-dissected films of infant–mother interactions. They found that both participants were closely involved in the exchanges, which changed on a second-by-second basis. It was here that they discovered the interactional sequence of harmony, disruption and repair, which has been identified as repeating in adult intimate relationships. Strikingly, they found that, on average, mothers correctly attune to their infant's emotional state only one-third of the time. This is seen when the baby is calm after their needs are correctly interpreted and satisfied. The rest of the time is spent in disruption and then repairing back to harmony again. The infant's response to the mis-attunement results in the mother's successful correction one-third of the time. The corrective behaviour is the mother's or carer's efforts to read the signals from the baby and to successfully intuit their needs. This constitutes the repair and is crucial in turning the child's feelings of despair into a more positive emotion, such as possibly relief or hope. The study concluded that successful repair attempts are essential for the infant's development and thus also for healthy intimacy between partners in adulthood.

In adult relationships, a similar cycle is observed. There is a lot more at stake for the adults in this cycle because, often, we unconsciously look for repair of adverse childhood experiences in the relationship with our partner. For this reason, relationships offer developmental and healing opportunities.

Co-regulation as repair

This repair process described above is known as co-regulating. It is something that babies and small children learn when they are soothed by loving carers because they cannot yet self-regulate or comfort themselves. They need the presence of a caring adult who can do that for them. The parent or carer regulates the child through eye contact, soothing sounds, empathic facial expressions, rocking, cooing or singing a lullaby to help them find peaceful equilibrium. Once their needs are met and any pain or discomfort has been reduced in this way, the baby or child becomes comforted and settles down. The calm person, the care-giver, is offering some of their calm to the baby or child who is upset, so that they can attune to their calm state.

In a less optimal situation a caregiver may not be able to self-regulate enough to be calm when the baby is in distress. They get stressed, over-react or under-react, and the baby gets more upset. This is dysregulation. In adults, this reveals itself when the person who is upset meets another and, instead of being soothed or reassured by them, the person they meet is unable to tolerate their distress and they too become upset. Instead of being affected in a positive way and moving towards ease, they move towards agitation, anxiety or distress. A negative emotional feedback loop is formed.

These processes of repair, attunement and connection are just as important in adult intimate relationships. We need to know we have the support of our partners and that they have our back. Committed relationships offer us a way to heal past ruptures through the present moment-to-moment process of relating with our partners. There is also an opportunity for growth in finding the necessary internal resources to manage the pain of the disruption and participate in the repair process. This process re-establishes the bond that was lost or compromised. The magnitude of the disruption will influence the size of the repair. When trust breaks or boundaries are breached, it will take longer to work through. If the hurt is intense or repetitive, the repair is not always possible. But for day-to-day disruptions, skills in repairing are essential to acquire. As relationships develop and individuals mature, repair work becomes more accessible and more necessary.

But inevitably, things go wrong. We miss a beat and inadvertently hurt our loved ones. The relationship only builds trust over time if we are available and willing to work through the disruptions and make successful repairs.

Bringing ever-greater consciousness and awareness to this cycle and the necessity of repair will help you to extend the length of time in the harmony phase.

The dynamics of relationship conflicts

'I am right, you are wrong'

Couples often argue over who's right and wrong. Or there are two different memories of the same event. Or two very different points of view over a situation. Perceived differences in values and morals can also cause splits and arguments. 'Your way is the wrong way' is the internal dialogue. 'Why don't you see it as I do?' These positions can become entrenched very quickly. We become stubborn in our viewpoint; it becomes an issue of pride, of self-identity that we stick to our own opinions. You're over there. I'm over here. The space between becomes an impasse.

'Normal marital sadism'

The psychologist David Schnarch coined the phrase 'normal marital sadism' to describe the subtle cruelty that can perpetuate in an ordinary, loving relationship. Of course, this cruelty is not what any couple would aim for, but in long-term relationships, it can start to happen gradually over time and takes work to undo.

Little put-downs, mean banter, unsympathetic reactions, remorseless bickering, just below all-out brutality. Also pretending we don't know what our partner wants – those moments when we know exactly what they would like, yet we ignore it and deny knowledge of it. These behaviours are culturally normalised: we see it in films, in our friends and relatives, and in ourselves at times. When we are angry and bitter, have low self-esteem or are in pain and hurting, we want to relieve the pain. So we put our partner down, criticise them, find fault, shed light on how inept and unworthy of our love they are. We blame them for being the source of our misery – 'If only they were different, I could be having a lovely life.'

There are so many 'ordinary' ways that we cause our partners to suffer. We avoid them, keep our distance, freeze them out, disconnect from physical contact and avoid eye contact. This pitilessness is subtle sadism. These can be standard everyday behaviours, yet these are the things that cause so much pain, resentment, hurt and anger. It can lead to alienation, suffering and relationship breakdown.

Criticism and defensiveness

Criticism between couples might be mild little nit-picking comments or outright disapproving judgements. Depending on the self-esteem of the criticised person, it'll either be – on a good day – helpful feedback or, at the other end of the scale, when we're feeling particularly vulnerable, utterly devastating. Criticism is anger that we express in a particularly pointed way when we are trying to get rid of a difficult feeling. It may come from our repressed longings – 'I can't bear this in myself, so I can't handle it in you.' We can't tolerate discomfort, so we tell our partners to behave differently.

We weigh negative aspects of what we hear more heavily than positive ones, so it is often better to leave minor irritations and criticisms unsaid, but this is so hard to do. Criticism usually comes from anxiety and obsessive impulses: the partner's tolerance levels are low and they resort to criticism in an attempt to get their partner to comply with their requirements. Criticism invites defensiveness. So if you criticise your partner, you can expect a defensive reaction and a negative cycle can easily escalate. Negativity is never a good way to produce change in your partner. Pointing out deficiencies may be tempting but rarely produces beneficial results, because negativity usually begets more negativity.

Research shows that partners get on best when they can manage the Herculean task of meeting negativity in a positive way. One way of doing this can be to try to understand your partner's unhappiness, recognising that they are not in a good place and might be feeling stressed or upset about something. Often, showing compassion for the other's difficulty helps the situation a lot. This requires the partner who is critical to move from a blaming and complaining stance to one that is more disclosing of their personal vulnerabilities. To blame others is a protective and offensive action that renders the complainer invulnerable. When the blamer can admit to their own difficulties by exposing their feelings and inner scripts, the things they might say to themselves about their own unworthiness or the other's behaviour which they don't like, it makes them more accessible and allows for more compassion to flow their way. Blaming and criticising often leads to negative conditioning, where you find the behaviour you don't want is reinforced in the other.

DEIRDRE AND CHANTAL

Deirdre and Chantal have been together for five years. When they initially met, they both felt they had found a kindred spirit; they share similar tastes, values and outlooks. Over the years, they realised they also share similar imprints in each other's backgrounds. Deirdre is often anxious; Chantal sees Deirdre as needing her support and help, in a similar way to how she helped her father after her parents separated. Deirdre initially saw in Chantal a supportive and strong person who gives her all the attention she needs. Chantal would often overhear her mother criticising and berating her father in the evenings after she had gone to bed. Chantal felt sorry for her browbeaten father and would leap to his defence and try to rescue him. As she got older, Chantal started to get the same critical treatment from her mother.

As the relationship develops, Deirdre complains of a constant sense of never having enough love, attention or understanding in her relationship with Chantal. Chantal forms a friendship with a co-worker in their community. Chantal talks openly about what is happening and maintains it is not a threat to how she feels towards Deirdre. But she begins to notice how Deirdre starts finding fault, complaining and criticising her. This reminds her of her mother and fills her with anger and resentment. Over the course of the next few months, arguments and fights become increasingly inflamed. The more Deirdre criticises, the more Chantal fights back, thinking that Deirdre is not taking responsibility for herself. This leaves Deirdre feeling more lost and resentful, and she fights more aggressively for the recognition she needs. The escalation in their fights continues until it becomes unbearable for them both. Chantal moves out for a while and they both seek help to work things through.

Deirdre works on finding better ways to manage her anger and learns to understand that she was dependent on Chantal to look after her and make up for the deficit of mothering as a child. Chantal sees how she was drawn into rescuing Deirdre because she had found a useful role for herself as a child in doing this for her father. The couple stay together and find compassion for what each of them was looking for in the other. They can still get triggered now and again, but are able to pull back from escalating the cycle because they know what drives it and have strategies for stepping off the ramp and de-escalating.

Violence and abuse

When someone is violent or abusive it is often symptomatic of their deep-seated fear, shame or feelings of inferiority and inadequacy. Being unable to accept these feelings in themselves, they act out violently in an attempt to eliminate them by conquering their source, which they see as the partner. Acting out violently also happens when negative thinking and persecutory internal scripts lead the person directly to violent behaviour without going through the mediating space of feelings. Impulses take over because of an inability to process thoughts in the feeling space between thinking and action.

In some relationships, one partner might deliberately provoke the other to act out violently. They might do this by using put-downs, jibes and goading in a bid to take them over the edge and thereby win moral superiority over them. As soon as they lose control and hit out, the other becomes the triumphant victim. Although the victim, they can now pronounce how terrible the other one is for losing control and thus they are able to belittle the partner even more. This is called 'persecuting from the victim position'. It comes from the Drama Triangle work developed by Dr Stephen Karpman. Partners might get stuck in any of the three positions of persecutor, rescuer or victim. A victim mentality will attract persecutors, a rescuer will attract victims and a persecutor will attract victims. It is rare to find two persecutors in a relationship, although it does happen. Such couples are known as hostile-detached and are often found to have a combative alliance where they are well matched and find their connection through combat. Relationship outcomes for hostile-detached couples are usually unsuccessful, according to research by the relationship research organisation, The Gottman Institute.

Another factor in violent relationships is co-dependency, where each one relies on validation by the other. In this kind of relationship, the violent partner will show remorse and contrition after the event and needs the forgiveness of the other partner to feel all right again. Because the non-violent partner relies on feeling needed by the violent partner, they willingly give their forgiveness as they fear leaving or being left if they don't. Some people choose violent partners so they can be the one to rescue and heal them. This is another form of co-dependent relationship, where each one serves a function for the other. This may sound surprising but people who do this might be unconsciously seeking to resolve a violent past with a satisfactory ending in the present. However, it rarely works and leads instead to a repetition of the same misery.

Another reason for partner violence can be disowned anger and aggression projected from the victim partner onto the aggressor partner. When one partner is unable to own their own aggression and anger, they can unconsciously attract a partner who holds it for them. This is why so many victims of violence stay with an aggressive partner. This is complicated by the real fear of the violent partner acting out more extremes forms of violence, should their partner try to leave. Or they may threaten violence against themselves, as in suicide.

The Gottman Institute defines two types of abuser: the pitbull type and the cobra type. Both can appear controlling. The pitbull is the one we refer to above who is anxious and dependent, who gets wound up easily and then can't control their emotions. They lose their temper but do not have at their core a wish to cause harm. They recognise afterwards that they have crossed a line and feel sorry for it. Anger management can often be helpful for this type of abuser. The cobra type is strategic and determined in menacing and abusive behaviour. They are unpredictable and do not show signs of remorse after an incident has occurred, or they make fake signs of remorse in order to manipulate. In such cases, one partner lives in a constant state of fear and vigilance of unprovoked attack.

Violence is never acceptable in relationships and if you are subject to violence, aggressive behaviour or verbal and emotional abuse, you should seek help immediately for your own safety. Emotional abuse includes intimidation, coercion, harassment, belittling, devaluing, making deprecating remarks, humiliating, shaming, or controlling behaviour.

When violence results from acting out heightened emotions generated through mutual provocation between partners, the matter can be treated by analysing triggers and reactive behaviours, and finding responses that are measured and considered. Unprocessed feelings, negative self-talk and inaccurate interpretations can also be worked through. In the interests of keeping both partners safe, a safety plan is devised with the therapist ready for implementation, should it be needed. This may range from partners identifying their own bodily early warning signals of emotional overwhelm, to establishing a code word for calling time out for cooling off, to having an overnight bag packed and a close friend or relative ready to receive you for an overnight stay.

The dynamics of relationship conflicts

A polarity exists when there are two opposing or contra-dicting views on a given subject or situation. You're over there seeing the world from your perspective and I'm over here with a very different view. When you're in an 'I'm right and you're wrong' argument with your partner, that is a polarity conundrum. Partners get entrenched in their end of the polarity and won't budge, which can lead to bitter disputes that arise repeatedly. That's another characteristic of a polarity: they are never solvable in a normal, rational way and are recurrent throughout the relationship.

Arguing about how to manage finances is a typical example. One of you is more cautious about spending money and wants to ensure there are savings to draw on. The other believes firmly in living for the day and is more extravagant with money. Another typical example could be anything around planning versus spontaneity.

One way that couples get stuck in polarised positions is the tendency to think of polarities as being unrelated, distinct and as separate from each other as two islands or planets. Yet they are intricately informed by each other and need one other to exist. There can be no concept of saving money without the concept of spending money; no idea of planning without the idea of spontaneity. As Carl Jung, the founder of analytical psychology, wrote in *Symbols of Transformation*, 'Every psychological extreme secretly contains its own opposite or stands in some sort of intimate and essential reaction to it. Indeed, it is from this tension that it derives its peculiar dynamism.'

So when we feel we are taking a completely opposing view to our partner, we need a *both/and* not an *either/or* approach. 'Finding a middle ground' can be a misnomer in relationships. What we need to do is to properly understand and take in the other's point of view. We allow the other to come into us, to let their perspective occupy us for a moment: to think about saving rather than spending money. Managing polarities in relationships means getting mobile and travelling to each other in thought, feelings and behaviour. The point of doing this is to validate your partner's view, hear their logic and acknowledge their truth, even if you don't share it or agree with it, thus closing the distance between the two of you. When you do this with an open mind and heart, something special can happen. There can be a completely new perspective through a union of opposites, which neither of you could see before. A third possibility becomes available that transcends both of the other positions. Jung called this process 'the transcendent function'. The tension of polarities happens both within each person, and between both person in the couple.

Trying to change your partner

'If only she would see it my way.' 'If only she were different.' 'If only he were more like me!'

Trying to manoeuvre our partner into being the person we want them to be can be a lifelong enterprise. We want them to change or to stay the same as we met. There's an enticing allure to the project as each of us thinks we are right, with the correct values, outlook and aspirations. But of course we protest when we feel pushed into being changed or adopting a different viewpoint. It can become a power struggle. We need to feel we have a choice and free will. That any change comes of our own volition. In trying to change your partner, you may simply force them into doing what you want. But this feels just as lousy as intolerance. No partner wants to comply any more than they want to be intolerant. For instance, you may feel more comfortable with a partner who is very vocal about their feelings, and demand that they share more about how they feel; they may comply, out of love for you, but it might come at the expense of their own emotional inner life, which might be quieter, more introspective. Asking for specific changes in behaviour is very different from wholesale change in personality.

When we feel this distance, and in those moments when our viewpoints and inner worlds feel poles apart with those of our partner, we need to find a middle way, a space between us that feels safe, where compromise and acceptance can occur. Creating a safe space through conversation and regular check-ins can be a healthy way to do this.

Judging and condemnation are things we do when we have been exhausted in our futile bid to change someone. Trying to change is what we do when we don't accept the situation at hand. Nothing will change unless we first accept the situation for what it is.

The 'two-choice dilemma'

If you want two things at the same time that are incompatible, it may be that you are experiencing what David Schnarch called 'two-choice dilemma'. Instead of transparency, you steal your partner's choice by concealing something, in order to have freedom to do our own thing.

For example, if one member of a couple in a monogamous relationship has an affair and keeps it secret. They want two things at once: to have the affair and stay in their relationship. Or perhaps someone wants to fix their marriage but not to have to change. You want more intimacy but you don't want to tolerate the anxiety of a closer connection. You want a heart-to-heart dialogue but you criticise your partner about the way they reveal their feelings. You want your partner to seduce you but you tell them they're not asking in the right way. We have the fantasy that we can make a choice that will avoid us being anxious. Yet, more likely, it is a choice between one anxiety or another. When a relationship is stuck or in a cycle of conflict, for it to move on and grow, change needs to happen. Often, the choice which feels the more challenging is likely to be the one that will bring most benefit.

The body, emotions and emotional responses to conflict

The body is a unified whole. Through our bodies we think, feel and act. These functions work together so seamlessly that it is difficult to differentiate a thought from an emotion from an impulse or a physical sensation. Emotion is not simply an isolated feeling. It is a combination of tendencies towards action, thoughts, feelings and sensations. For instance, we might have an immediate feeling of wanting to get out of a situation, to move away. Or we may feel the opposite, that we want to move in and resolve things. We generate little scripts that we say to ourselves, such as 'this is hopeless' or 'I'm being gaslit here', which then produce further feelings. Feelings are felt through the body in distinct sensations.

Emotions help us adapt to situations by giving us the felt sense of response. Our heart rate rises, we heat up, our breathing changes and we might sweat or have digestion changes. All of these physical responses are clues to the emotion we're feeling. Sometimes we don't know which emotion it is, we just know we're feeling something. Emotions help us survive by providing an efficient rapid response in critical situations – drawing back, pausing, looking around. They also prepare us for action – stepping forward, speaking up, getting clear. Also, they help us make a plan of action – reassessing, taking a break, redefining boundaries and trying something new.

Avoiding uncomfortable emotions

From huge fiery fights to frosty freeze-outs, some couples struggle with emotional control. Some people try to balance by pulling back from too much emotion or they fear overwhelm, so rebalance with rationality. A familiar dynamic around emotion is that partners fear triggering emotions in each other. They don't want to rock the boat, as they worry it will bog the relationship down, hold them up and keep them from the bliss of harmony they want so desperately. The truth is the opposite. If an emotion is uncomfortable, one that we'd prefer not to feel, it's human nature to avoid it, skim over it or skip to something else if possible. We're all looking for comfort and habituated to turning away from discomfort.

But avoiding or suppressing emotion lays tracks for later explosions and engulfment.

CARLY AND SAM

Carly and Sam are so 'nice' to each other. They are softly spoken, kind and gentle; they keep things calm and happy between them. They both admit to avoiding difficult emotions, fearing it will plunge them into trouble and strife. Carly fears her emotions might drive Sam away from her, so she represses her anxiety and tries to hide it from him. Whenever she brings anything emotional into focus, his anxiety spikes, so he actively supports her in repressing her emotion. He encourages her to 'chill out' with alcohol. They have a few beers while watching TV. But being busy doing things is Carly's way of managing her anxiety and also a more comfortable way to show her care for Sam. Whenever they get space to talk, they stay in safe territory and veer away from anything difficult. Deep down, she feels his emotional needs are enormous compared to hers and she worries that she can't possibly meet them. But this strategy of avoidance reduces intimacy and drives them further from each other in the long term. Their particular stress, which neither want to face, is their infertility issue. While they both manage to keep things calm between them most of the time by suppressing emotion, their attempts ultimately fail. Every so often, there is a 'Vesuvius' eruption in the relationship and everything blows.

One day, a realisation comes to Carly that changes the course of the relationship. She visits her mother to tell her about their infertility problem and how this is causing such unhappiness in her relationship. Her mother pours a glass of wine and Carly nervously launches into the difficulties and how she thinks they will need to get IVF treatment. To Carly's disbelief, her mother immediately changes the subject by pointing out the beautiful motifs in the crystal-cut glasses they are drinking from. Carly is reminded how she could never talk to her mother about anything personal and that she has inherited and is perpetuating this awkward avoidance around emotive subjects. Later, she sees how even her choice of partner was governed by her own emotional avoidance. Sam is a perfect fit for her because of his anxiety around emotional issues and techniques for avoidance dovetail with hers.

The process of naming and feeling emotion is something Carly and Sam are at first reluctant to explore because it feels so alien to them. But they have come to see that suppressing and trying to control the uncontrollable results in further turmoil with their big eruptions. They understand that there is nothing to fear in expressing their feelings and that neither of them would run away. As a result, their life begins to take on more colour and dynamism as they can talk more freely without the need for diversionary tactics. They are able to address their infertility issues, to support each other through treatment and reach out for help when they need it. Their alcohol consumption also reduces as they are less invested in avoiding their feelings.

Recognising the effects of trauma

We all have issues, situations or abuses that we wish hadn't happened. What happened in our past cannot be changed. But we can change how we approach our feelings to it in the present moment. Current events trigger past trauma and yet the response resides in our bodies, in the nervous system, not in the past event. The innate wisdom of the body provides an exit when it is needed. Feelings can be closed down, numbed or split off. We can become vacant, absent, spaced out, disengaged with our bodies. Being absent can be a refuge. Emotional compartmentalising can be self-preservation, a creative way of protection. Sometimes we disconnect because there is too much information, or it is too fast, or too soon, or too confusing.

Disconnection is how the trauma survivor has managed to cope. It may have been a helpful defence and it might still be useful, or it may be a habit we no longer need. In relationships, a partner with a trauma adaptation might close down around specific emotional subjects or shut their partner down when those subjects arise, causing one partner to be unavailable to the other on an emotional level. These adaptations can raise problems in relationships, which will need some care, attention, understanding and kindness.

Instead of pushing away the uncomfortable feelings, which build resistance, chasms and walls, we can learn incrementally to be with the feelings and sensations in the present moment. It doesn't necessarily mean continually revisiting the trauma, it is about meeting those places in ourselves to get familiar with them, to be with them in the present rather than pushing them away.

Our bodies have a miraculous capacity to repair. For example, a callus forms around a fracture as 'threads' of bone cells start to grow. When our skin is wounded, it forms granulation tissue. As it heals, the wound gets smaller. On a physical level, our bodies have a fantastic ability to convalesce, recover and mend our way back to total health. This ability of the body to heal is echoed in how healing can take place in a healthy relationship. When relational wounds are left to fester, resentment and bitterness can build, leading to isolation and separation, making repair much more difficult.

Managing emotions

To repair conflicts, we will need to learn to recognise old patterns of relating and practise new patterns that generate 'good conflict'. Good conflict leads to breakthroughs rather than breakdowns. A repair may be very complex and painstaking, such as following infidelity or abandonment, or less extreme, like forgetting a milestone anniversary, being dismissive of an illness or arriving late for a date. Far from catastrophe, although it might seem like that at the time, these are golden opportunities for the critical repair process. Without repair, there can be no development.

Managing our emotions, without either getting over-whelmed them or avoiding them altogether, is critical. When our partner is angry with us, acknowledging their anger without needing to shut them down or escalate is a foundation of good conflict. Fighting fair means not being aggressive or blaming but expressing emotions responsibly. Then your partner won't need to defend themself or make a counterattack, but instead can validate your anger and respond from their place of being grounded and centred. Though it gets tricky when we cycle the same conflict in repetitive, hurtful ways and when we trigger each other's core wounds. These tend to be things like a sense of not being enough, being unlovable or feeling inferior in some way – stupid, dirty, unwanted or ugly. Whatever it is, it will influence how you behave, particularly when challenged.

As human beings, we seek pleasure and turn away from pain and discomfort. In the same way we look for the comfy spot on the sofa, we'll lean into the easy places in ourselves and in our relationships. When change occurs, the places in ourselves that we have been avoiding – our hurts, wounds, insecurities, vulnerabilities – can be touched upon and we make subtle, private, often unconscious choices as to how we manage these. Often we circumnavigate our discomfort and pain by blaming, criticising, poking and prodding our nearest and dearest. The way to reduce 'normal marital sadism' is to feel our own feelings and to allow ourselves to be vulnerable.

How do we go towards vulnerability? It helps to know we are not alone. It's likely at some time someone else has felt this feeling or has been through something as bad. Most likely even in the precise moment, as we ourselves are feeling it. When we see our own problems reflected in the stories of others, we suddenly feel less alone.

Self-soothing and self-regulation

You cannot leave a place until you have fully arrived there. Emotion must first be accepted, allowed to be felt by you, allowed to have its lifespan through your body. It helps to know there's a reason for it, as most of us can tolerate discomfort if we know it will lead to an easier or better life, somewhere down the line. Self-regulation and co-regulation are a pre-requisite for this to happen. Self-regulation is how we manage to regulate our own moods and anxiety. Self-soothing is the actions we take to regulate ourselves, which we learn as adults. These actions might include going for a walk or a run, lying down or stretching, listening to soothing music or breathing deeply and slowly. We give further suggestions below. Co-regulation is how another person's physical and emotional presence can help us regulate. For co-regulation, you might reach out to your partner or a friend or seek the support of a therapist or counsellor.

The intimacy of two people in a harmonious relationship can result in the feeling of an oppressive bond for some people. Engulfment or abandonment are the two primary fears of childhood. There can be various reasons and triggers for dysregulation and everyone is different. People who have experienced aggression, danger and trauma in the past may be more prone to being triggered. When triggered, everyone will have their own specific indicators of emotional flooding and it's important to see if you can identify yours. The body needs at least 20 minutes to re-regulate from emotional flooding.

When we are suffering emotional overwhelm, our heartrate increases, stress hormones cortisol and adrenaline are released and the body goes into fight, flight or freeze mode in response to perceived danger. Heightened emotions and negative thoughts create an influx of physiological sensations. There could be a tightness in the throat, sweaty palms, a narrowing of hearing or visual field. In all cases, it is impossible to think clearly. At this point, people behave in different ways according to their attachment style. Some get defensive, become angry and fight, others stonewall and shut down in freeze, and a few will turn away and walk out in a flee response. Usually there's a mixture of all of these behaviours accompanied by strong emotions.

We need to be able to hold onto ourselves and find ways to self-regulate. This means being calm, having flexibility and having empathy for yourself and others. When someone is self-regulated, they have a sense of being well-adjusted and can manage their behaviour appropriately. They are available for connection and can engage in a balanced way, being co-operative, perhaps with some good humour, while also maintaining good boundaries.

Self-soothing helps us to self-regulate. Take a deep breath, bringing awareness to the inhale or exhale. Find a sense of being anchored in the body or try any other similar way you find soothes you (we give some examples on the following page). Sometimes it can work to bring attention to our sensations, any sensation. What we see, hear, taste, smell or touch. Like a moment of meditation, of taking yourself in, noticing how you are, here and now. It helps us calm the mind, but intentional breathing alters us physiologically by lowering our heart rate, which helps the body recover from an automatic fight or flight response. A lower heart rate sends signals back to the brain that there is no danger or threat to life.

The good news is that human bodies are amazing at self-regulating and there are many techniques we can learn to support self-regulation. Through repetition of simple body awareness techniques we accumulate a body memory, which means the next time we need to self-regulate our bodies remember, we develop a capacity for it. All of these simple suggestions will help you to self-regulate by giving attention to sensations in the present moment. Do one at a time or just choose one that works for you and repeat it whenever needed:

- Feel the connection your body has with the chair
- Feel the connection your feet have with the ground
- Take a deep breath and give attention to the sensation of the breath
- Relax your shoulders
- Soften the muscles in your forehead, in your jaw, in your belly
- Look around you; notice the colours, shapes and textures
- Give attention to each of the senses, what you can see, hear, smell, touch or taste.

Hopefully, as you read this, you might have tried one or two of them. You may notice a difference in your own connection with yourself.

Co-regulation and touch

As you soothe yourself, the next step is to emotionally reach out to your partner by expressing your feelings and seeking repair as necessary. When we help each other to soothe and self-regulate, this is called co-regulation.

Co-regulation happens when the person who is agitated is soothed by being close to the calmer person. We can actually be healers for each other by increasing our own self-regulation and being available in a relationship to share that calm when the situation needs it. When we relax and breathe fully, we are fully aware of all our senses. The heartbeat goes down and we are able to be spontaneous. People in this state can have fun and play. Co-regulation is a 'mood contagion', where heartbeat lowers and we breathe more without even needing to be aware of what is happening.

Co-regulation is a continuous and dynamic process whereby we affect our partners and are affected by them. Given that, as humans, we're looking for balance and equanimity in our lives, co-regulation takes precedence over dysregulation. The more emotionally secure partner stabilises the other to feel more comfortable – akin to a good host at a party who is so welcoming that you relax and enjoy the evening. This dynamic plays out in a relationship without either person being consciously aware.

We all need other people, that is the nature of being human. Human beings have evolved to function well with the support of others. When we are in partnerships, family and communities, among people who are well-adjusted, validating and co-operative, we have increased resiliency and potential for optimal growth and wellbeing.

Accept that your partner isn't perfect

The 'utopia' mindset hopes for someone who can tick all the boxes. They're gorgeous, kind, sexy, funny, generous, intelligent and compassionate. They have integrity, share our values, speak several languages and have great dress sense. We're looking for 100 per cent compatibility, the light of my life. Yet, in reality, there's an 80/20 rule. If 80 per cent of them is good enough, then that's plenty. The other 20 per cent you can ignore. When they tune the radio to a channel you don't like, when they leave their empty mug on the table and the toothbrush in the wrong place. If all their annoying foibles only add up to 20 per cent of them, then overlook it. Silently categorise it as 'a 20 per cent thing' and move on.

Or it might not be about them, but about your relationship – that they're grumpy in the mornings so can't discuss the day in the way you'd like, or they're stubborn in the argument about the sofa, or they're unhelpful when your family comes to stay. Those things about how you relate together that might rumble on for years. But again, if they make up 20 per cent of the relationship or less, find a way to tolerate it. Soften around it so that you don't end up brittle and put your attention on the 80 per cent.

If 80 per cent of your relationship is good enough, then it's a good enough relationship. Within that 80 per cent, there will still be issues that need addressing; it doesn't all have to be a perfect 80 per cent, but harmonious enough, pretty OK and fun much of the time.

When we find the courage to accept what is happening in our lives and relationships, instead of labelling, theorising, complaining or fighting against it, we can more readily get to work finding solutions. Acceptance takes courage because it can be a surrender to the movement of our lives, which is often beyond our control. But relinquishing control frees up energy that can be reassigned from blaming to problem solving.

Confront the problems

But where there are problems which cause deep division, rather than the 20 per cent of niggles which might cause minor annoyance, they need to be addressed. Every relationship will have its own set of problems. No relationship is problem-free. Understanding that conflict is part of being human can help us tolerate and accept the difficulties, at which point we can discover creative solutions and find the middle ground.

In a relationship, there are going to be issues that trip you up again and again. They could be minor issues that will be a bit controversial, are not major sources of division but might cause small conflicts from time to time. For instance: you've got a hankering to change your family holiday plans, you've noticed how good-looking the new person in the office is, you felt dismissed by your partner at that party last week. Ignoring these stumbling blocks is more dangerous as they stay in the background and limit the possibilities for communication. If you dodge one, before you know it, others will appear and you'll be hopping around trying to avoid them all, exhausting yourself and unable to go anywhere. So, at the first opportunity, face it square on. Move towards the difficult conversation.

Addressing those sticky issues helps us grow tolerance towards disputes and disconnection. They'll be the tricky conversations about money and chores, the intimate conversations about sex and desire, the vulnerable discussions about life's purpose and meaning. These tender areas are the places to go into and talk about all the more. It can feel counter-intuitive. Why would we want to do that if we're getting along well enough? Why risk rocking the boat? Because eradicating disparities is, first of all, not possible, but also it is not healthy. We can acknowledge that we don't see things the same way, and it's OK. We can learn to tolerate our own, separate emotional worlds and celebrate differences.

Learn to hold the tension of opposites

One of the challenges of managing our internal polarities is first to recognise that they exist. All our character traits have an opposite. For instance, if you consider yourself to be a generous or altruistic person, you must also acknowledge that you also contain the capacity to be selfish or stingy. To be in a mature, passionate relationship is to find gradual mobility on our continuums, rather than getting stuck in either pole or switching from one end to the other.

When someone denies, disowns or doesn't acknowledge the existence of one pole of an attribute in themselves, they might vilify their partner for having it. This is known as splitting. A person who is proud and denies their own shame splits it off and points out things in you that you might feel shameful about, or they highlight any faults of yours where they might feel a lack of worth. A person who always appears to be calm and collected and points out how anxious you are is denying their own anxiety. Instead of holding the tension of the polarity of calmness and anxiety within themselves, they split off one half of the polarity, in this case the anxiety, and accuse you of being the anxious one.

Polarities need to be accepted and owned in their completeness with us and not split between you and your partner. Acknowledging you have both aspects of polarities in you is taking responsibility for your personal development. Relationships can bring about healing and repair when we realise that we have been fighting and deny aspects of ourselves and projecting them onto our partner.

When we let someone else into our lives, this might include acknowledging and owning the things we don't like about ourselves and finding ways to integrate them and be kind to ourselves.

Shifting perspective to find balance

Relationships constantly adjust to find stability and balance, just like a thermostat keeps the room at a given temperature. Turning the thermostat dial up or down, depending on the weather outside, applies more or less heat to maintain a steady level. In relationships, there is an equivalent, known as a 'first order change'. During an argument, this is an ineffective way of trying to find balance. Partners turn the dial up or down on each other, either getting louder and starting to shout in a bid to be heard and to get their point acknowledged, or they go silent, withdraw and stonewall. The latter is seen in passive-aggressive behaviours, when one or both partners are silently fuming but not admitting it. This might show up as sarcasm, back-handed compliments which criticise, procrastination, resistance or withdrawing. These strategies are attempts to regulate the relationship through first order change but they will always prove unsatisfactory.

This game-without-end might be familiar to you. It is a negative feedback loop – that sense of going around the same highly frustrating argument and not finding a way out, for days, months or years. It is known as the 'attack/defend pattern': one attacks, the other defends and both hold each other in an endless loop of wanting to be right and make the other wrong. This is a classic first order change attempt to win superiority, to bring the other person down while raising yourself up. It's important to realise that you are both responsible for this situation, or 'game', because the moves you make are provocatively pulling the other partner into the dynamic in an irresistible way. This is a zero sum game. Neither of you win.

However, in a second order change perspective, partners recognise the 'game' they are playing. They see that right and wrong are polarised positions and that engaging in a power struggle is hopeless. They realise that the way to achieve change is to stop playing the game. In the metaphor of the thermostat, instead of turning the dial up or down on each other in a bid to regulate the heat in the room, they get out of the room and change the programme on the heating system. The ability to alter the pattern is powerful.

When we see the hostile dynamic as a pattern, we can change it. For instance, it might be enough to simply say: 'Hey, we're stuck in that circular fight again. I don't want to blame and attack you. Let's stop.' The source of the problem then shifts location from your opponent to the fight itself. You then both become a team looking at finding a solution to the negative pattern. In couple relationships, bringing awareness to how each of you tries to regulate the relationship is empowering and helps bring understanding in finding new ways to meet each other.

When do you call it quits?

For relationships to function healthily, both partners must be clear about making a voluntary choice to opt in. This choice needs to be made again and again; when the heat is turned up, when division and unhappiness are encountered, your partner needs to know that you are staying because you want to stay, not because you have to stay. When there is any form of compulsion to stay – for instance, because you don't have resources of your own, or you stay for the kids, or because you have low self-esteem and are afraid of being alone – this is likely to destabilise the relationship. No partner can be truly content knowing you stay with them because you cannot leave.

This leads some to test each other on this basis, wanting to know how much their partner really wants them. They might start pushing boundaries to see if the other partner will leave or not. If the partner threatens to leave, they can feel reassured that they are a voluntary choice. But if the partner is patient and kind and tolerates the acting out behaviour, the other is not reassured because they feel they are left with no doubt that the partner is staying out of desperation and not choice. Whichever way it goes, once the status quo returns, doubts set in again. This can lead to an oscillation between partners separating and getting back together again. To resolve this distressing pattern, both partners need to go deeper into their own issues for better mutual understanding.

Our story

Conflict and arguments in a relationship are normal. Knowing this was a big help for us. Instead of feeling we were failing, we could feel assured that perhaps there was nothing really wrong with either of us. We used to have big blow-outs where we would name-call and be horrid to each other. Sarah's way of coping would be to get more explosive and Matt's way was to eventually shut down and sulk for days. Now we are more fluent in the art of arguing. We are fairer to each other in our fights. But there is still a memory of those old positions which beckon to us when we are hurt.

At times of conflict for Matt, there is a body-memory of the shut-down state, which feels hopeless and stuck, as if the lights have been turned out. At these times, Sarah can feel the call of wanting to raise her voice in frustration. These two positions are the opposite of the traits we tend to display most often, where Matt is more the octopus, the one to move towards connection, and Sarah is the turtle, moving away to be alone. This messiness was only possible to get out of after we had been in it for a long time, trying to find the door.

The repetition, which we called our hamster wheel, came about because we were always applying the same failing techniques in our efforts to gain the upper hand on the other, to be right and justified. This is the first order change – all we were doing was turning the temperature of the argument (the game) up or down. It was like playing ping-pong faster or slower. This game always started with the sure conviction in each of us that we would be the winner. There was a great sense of gratification in that to begin with. Matt would sulk, telling himself that he knew better and was the poor, misunderstood victim at the mercy of this terrible woman. Sarah would tell herself she was the victor and living with an ill-informed simpleton. But after playing this game for several years, it began to dawn on us that actually neither of us was the winner. We were both losers. It was most definitely not gratifying.

Why did it take us so long to see this? Because we were matching up to each other in a power struggle, each trying to defend our own sense of self. We believed there was one truth and you either had it or you didn't. We thought we should both see the same truth. This meant we were merged. We could not differentiate and allow the other to have their own views, feelings and thoughts. There was no third body to inhabit in the space between us, from which we could observe and have curiosity and wonder at how different and beautifully unique we each are and how valuable each of our contributions are.

Thankfully, after years of the same old game, we now usually manage to stop it after the first round, or at least before half-time. We give each other the benefit of the doubt. If we disagree, we point out plainly without blame. We say so if we think the other is being unreasonable or intransigent, and we are more able to hear this alternative point of view from the other without feeling it as a blow to our self-esteem. We can shift more quickly into positive mood, laugh about our insecurities and sometimes maladaptive ways of coping with them.

Ways to interrupt the game, to bring about a second order change, where the game itself is identified as the problem, are many and varied. You will find what works for you. For us it was humour, some physical touch, a tickle or a fun poke in the ribs. This would not have worked before we were aware of 'the game'. But now we are, it serves as a light-hearted reminder to put down the rackets.

Exercises

The ball, in the metaphor of a game of tennis, goes from me to you. It could be a conversation, an argument, or in lovemaking. You say this or do this, I counter it or compliment it by saying that or doing the other. Do we contribute to it or denigrate it? While you do yours, I'm partly focused on my sentence or move ready to lob back to you. But when we pull back the focus and see the bigger picture, we see the whole game. It's an odd sensation, a bit like realising the film you're watching is a film, as if the microphone comes into view, or you see a camera almost out of frame, or the actor reading their lines. It blows the cover, it breaks the suspension of belief and we get to see it for what it truly is. Then we have more choices, we're not lost in our reactions, we can have an overview. What do you want to do next? Keep arguing? Or have a cuddle instead? Keep discussing the topic? Keep the same lovemaking moves that you've been doing for years? Or get creative and explore something unknown? Switching sides in an argument can help you see the game you are playing and rise above the content. It also demonstrates to your partner what you know about their argument, and this can be reassuring.

Switch Sides

This is one of our golden gems that we've established in our relationship. 'Walk in my shoes' – literally. See the world from their side. It's an experiment. It's playful; you don't know what's going to happen. It's also an intervention, pausing the flow of the argument to try something different. We offer it to you to use when you have disagreements, arguments and conflicts. It's particularly useful when these are entrenched, repetitive, divisive and exasperating, and just rumble on in some way. Most of us have got one or two of those lurking in the wardrobe.

We've been playing 'switch sides' for many years. It evolved from a few different strands. We have some arguments that have recycled and regurgitated for what feels like millennia. They get so well established, it's like we're just running a script, round and round in the same utterly exasperating circles. As the proverb goes: 'Necessity is the mother of invention', and we invented 'switching sides'.

It requires an ability to 'keep your eye on the ball, not the game'. To call 'time out' mid argument, to pause and change perspective. Instead of focusing on who said what and how much it hurt, it encourages you to draw back and look at the interaction as a whole. We were also inspired by experiencing the 'two chair work' of Gestalt psychotherapy, where the client will move from chairs representing different perspectives or different aspects of themselves. The ability to inhabit a different position is at the same time extraordinary and familiar.

We have offered this to clients in sessions and in our workshops. When couples can relinquish their positions in a locked binary system of 'my view' (which is right) and 'your view' (which is wrong), it often brings a great sense of freedom and the 'third way' will unlock, revealing itself as a possibility. It can be surprisingly easy to really inhabit the other view. Often it is fun, and sometimes quite funny. It takes courage and flexibility, and aids differentiation.

To start with, you need to be in two opposing positions, taking opposing views or arguing different sides of an argument. When you first try this, it can help to practise on an argument, conflict or discussion that is very familiar to you; one that you've recycled many times. The one about the furniture, or the finances, or the flirtations, one where you know their 'lines' quite well. Once you both know how to play 'switch sides', you can get more adventurous and play it in the midst of a fresh disagreement.

Once you've both agreed this is what you will do, have an objective look at the position your partner is standing in, their posture, gesture. You're going to have to recall the tone of voice and all physical mannerisms they were using while in this argument, as well as what they were actually saying.

Then, swap positions with your partner. Literally go where they are and they go where you are – get up, move places, switch over. Put your body where their body was – the location as well as the position. If they were standing by the fridge with their arms crossed and chin raised, go do that. If you were leaning on the counter with slouched shoulders and your hands in your pockets, your partner takes that position. Be as precise as you can with the details, the muscle tone, direction of eye gaze. As you hold this position, you might start to feel a little of what it's like to be them.

Then start talking as if you held your partner's opinions. This can be remarkably challenging. It not only requires you to have really listened to their argument in the first place, but then for you to say the words that they said. It requires you to put aside your original side of the argument and speak as if you were them. Even though, of course, you both disagree with the words coming out of your own mouths. It can be helpful to remember at this point that you're doing this as an experiment, and to bear in mind the goodwill involved to get a different perspective on your argument.

Can you attempt to see your partner's outlook? While you speak these words and hold this position, have a look at them. There they are, attempting to 'be you' – even if you think they look silly or sound ridiculous or aren't quite 'getting you' perfectly, can you take in, even slightly, this mirror that they hold for you? It can help you to be more objective about your own view. It also helps you to know you are understood and validated by your partner. You see that they actually do perceive and comprehend your point of view. By standing in their shoes, can you get a glimpse of their world and feel into the experience of their standpoint? Notice what it's like for you in this place.

If you're having difficulty being them, you can switch sides again, going back to your original positions and arguing from the original standpoints. Then, switch again when you have absorbed a little more of their side. When you switch, don't try to be yourself in their shoes, you are being them in their shoes. So, don't try to bring in your side of the argument when you have switched: if you deliberately distort the other's view, make fun of it or trivialise it, this may inflame the situation. To make this work, just keep to whatever viewpoint they had. Stick to saying their words as if it were a script.

Having switched positions and really inhabited the other polarity, consider if there is a 'third way'. Something neither of you had thought of before. It often is glaringly obvious, yet neither were able to see it when you were stuck fighting your corner.

The realisation follows that what was keeping you stuck was staying in a position you were comfortable with relative to your partner. The third way is an ideal solution. You have found it together; it includes both of your values and there is no winner or loser. You have both given up your rigid positions and been able to find this third way, which may have aspects of each position or none. It arises out of a completely new coalition between partners.

PART 3

Building Eroticism and Love in The Space Between Us

7

The Third Body

'The interplay of two polarities calls forth a third, which is the "mediating" or "reconciling" principle between them.'
– CYNTHIA BOURGEAULT

The third body lives in the space between us

1+1=3. This is clearly not mathematically correct, but biologically and synergistically, it is. In an intimate relationship, the additive sum of one plus one can bring about a biological third, as in a baby. Likewise, a couple can bring a third into existence synergistically. Synergy is the result of an interaction of two elements that brings about a combined effect greater than the sum of the individual elements. When a couple can synthesise the divisive polarities that are inherent in their relationship, a synergistic effect is produced which gives energy and vitality to the relationship and each person in it. As an example, the powerful force between negative and positive polarities creates the third element of electricity. This transcends the two poles of negative and positive and is far greater than the sum of them both. So it can also be in a couple relationship. If managed well, a polarity offers the opportunity for synergy through the synthesis of the two poles, which produces the third element to transcend them both. Yet most of the time, this doesn't happen without effort and struggle.

The third body is a perspective that is alive between two people in a relationship. A relationship is a system. A system is a collection of elements, which includes human beings that work together with a single purpose. Together, they produce a mechanism or interconnecting network, which is complete in itself. It involves two people who work together to create a relationship.

Any system created out of two entities is inherently unstable. Think of a bicycle, for instance: it's only stable when it is moving in one direction. If there is any uncertainty about the direction of travel, a bicycle will wobble when movement slows and fall over when it stops. A tricycle, on the other hand, is stable, whether moving or not. A two-person system of the couple is similar. If the couple are engaged on a plan, have a motive, are moving and are of one mind, the relationship can work. But as soon as there is difference to contend with, gridlock sets in. Decisions can't be made, things don't happen, conflict ensues. A couple becomes unstable through the inability to synthesise a polarity; a third object or person is sought to stabilise the disordered system and relieve the pressure and frustration of gridlock and inaction. But with the right skills and mindset, the couple can bring about the reconciling third between them to transcend inevitable polarities and support the relationship, obviating the need for any of the maladaptive behaviours that often beset relationships. Managing polarities is the most fundamental challenge of being in a relationship. Every couple will know this to some degree or another.

The relationship is a third product of two subjective worlds. It is a vantage point each of you can step into and see you both engaging together in the relationship. It is the 'idea' of the relationship. It is the sphere of the dream space, the imaginal. This has huge power. We can see this stability in engineering: a triangle creates stability, solidity and the potential to withhold substantial pressure. Each person has an internalised view of themselves, the other and the relationship between the two. Holding a concept of a third position is essential to overcome and transcend divisiveness which is caused when we only think in terms of the *either/ or* of two polar positions. By engaging in *both/and* thinking, exploring the opposite position of your partner, even though you may abhor every aspect of it, a synergistic process can arise, showing you both the superior third way.

In the material world, the third body can be the home you create together, which literally becomes your third body as it houses you both together. It's important that both partners feel equally invested in creating the home environment so that both can feel it is a comfortable and inviting space, a shared sanctuary. Other aspects might be a shared bank account, tableware or photograph album. Something to say 'this is ours'. Life itself is created; we might start a family, our extended family overlaps, we build community. And then there is the realm of imaginative space, of desire, dreams and potential. Sharing memories, secrets and plans. What do you want to achieve as a couple? What do you stand for? What are your values and outlook on the world? In all these ways, we can tend to the third body and it becomes a useful resource for each of you in the relationship.

There is a motivational force within each individual. It is the inner aspect of each of us that has desires, wishes and hopes in life. Aristotle referred to this as 'entelechy', which basically means 'life force'. It is able to witness itself and is the part that recognises experience and can comment on it. It is the ability to say 'I'. A relationship between two people is consequently formed from those two individuals each with their own life force that make three components: me, you and us. When we bond with another and become part of us, it can feel as if our choices are being limited and our freedom curtailed.

There might be challenges in steering a path between doing what you want to do and committing to a relationship. This is where the third body is needed. When two people join together, there can be a shared destination, often unknown at the time of meeting, mediated through the third body that also has its own life force. The third body is the unknown, until it comes into existence and we see what it is. When you join together, you must necessarily, therefore, also join the unknown. Once you are joined, then you develop and shape it, and begin to make it into something known to both of you. Both of your individual evolutions join forces with the third as it evolves with you. There will always be unknowns between you, but they become something to be curious about and explore together; they become imprinted with the language of your relationship and carry you along. 'Us' has its own being as the life force of the relationship. It is an indivisible unit with its own flavour, texture and ambience that can either be neglected or tended with love.

When the third body is held in mind and nurtured, it can become a space between you where each of you can feel liberated to unfold and develop your potential together in the relationship.

The third body is the palpable atmosphere between two people that we might gauge if we walk into a room, whether they're loving or arguing. It is the attentiveness of that couple to the space between them, the way it is cultivated, nurtured and cherished. Honest communication and fluency of repairing disruptions strengthen and cherish the third body. Tending to it is like taking care of anything you love – giving it attention and being grateful for the enjoyment it brings. Small gestures add up to a bigger totality. We put in positive actions not merely for you or me but for the relationship, which is, after all, our creation. A healthy and vibrant third body is the difference between two individuals just going along side by side, and two people with a strong, intimate connection, creating a loving atmosphere of kindness, joy and support.

In the process of making the relationship, two individuals face the challenge of creating a shared goal for the relationship that embraces the will of both of them. This shared goal becomes part of the third body; it has its own being, trajectory, potency and momentum.

Finding the third way can be painful because it requires a developmental change in the individual. We do this by reconciling and integrating aspects of ourselves that we have disowned. The good news is that we're always changing. The self is always in metamorphosis and never static. Every crisis requires us to examine who we think we are and often negate our present state in order to find a new possibility of being in a relationship. Another way of putting this is to stand down from an egocentric position and be receptive to the needs of the other and the present moment. The potential of human development is always in a state of flux and never a finite process. It is always emerging into new possibilities, created when there is a commitment to nurture and care for the third body.

The third body perspective sees the relationship as more important than one or other of the individuals being right. When you have the willingness to stay present with what you want without being aggressive, the third way can become apparent. Instead of 'my way or the highway', it's neither your way nor my way but the way of the third body. This requires both to stay present in the process of negotiating, like holding hands and looking at the problem together. Then something beyond the self can emerge.

The third body is shared meaning and understanding

Relationships need at least some conflict. Then, through the voicing of different opinions, values and outlooks, differences can be negotiated and new outcomes reached. This makes a relationship dynamic and alive. But polarisation, when you and your partner get stuck in differing viewpoints and oppose each other, can be bitter and miserable. When our views turn into a dichotomy, the two sides become increasingly antagonistic, expressing mistrust and suspicion. I am right and you are wrong. How come they don't get it?

Shared meaning is necessary for successful dialogue. For this to be achieved, we need to put aside our own opinions and allow ourselves to find a shared understanding. We need to suspend our thinking sometimes in order to allow us to see how our problems are often generated by our thoughts. 'That's his view and this is mine,' is a false dichotomy.

When you argue because you see things differently, or remember something differently, it's helpful to keep in mind that neither of you is seeing the whole picture, but only part of the whole. The truth of anything is too large to be contained in only one body. Together, you know more than either of you could alone. Think of those optical illusion drawings where you can either see a duck or a rabbit within one picture, depending on whether you look at the foreground or the background first, or discern two faces either side of a vase in the middle. When looking at these sorts of pictures, you can't see both at the same time. Sometimes it can take a while to be able to see the other figure, but when you do, it's an 'ah ha' moment, like a light going on. Once seen, you can't un-see it. And when you have seen them both, you can shift between seeing one or the other by using your attention.

In a relationship, it's like one of you is seeing one figure and the other is seeing the other. Both are correct but neither of you can see both. Each of you feels you are right in your assertion of what you see. Each of you is seeing part of the whole accurately but neither of you is seeing the whole picture. But the third body holds the potential for both images to be seen at the same time, which is impossible for either of you to do individually.

JAKE AND DAPHNE

Jake and Daphne have just moved into their new flat together. Jake has a lovely old leather Chesterfield sofa. He'd had it for years in his own flat before he met Daphne. Daphne doesn't think it fits in very well. It's quite long and they argue about where to put it. Jake favours one position, Daphne another. They get really heated about it. Jake moves the room around so the sofa is in the position he prefers. Next day, Daphne moves it back. This goes on for a while. They can't believe how stupid the other is not to see their point of view. They wonder if this is the beginning of the end of their relationship, whether the other's major personality flaws are emerging through their stubbornness. Jake uses his best logic to convince Daphne of why his position works better. She 'knows' that he is wrong and she is right.

After several exasperating weeks, tired and forlorn, they both surrender to the situation and fling themselves on the sofa in despair. 'Tell me what it means to you, Jake?' says Daphne, in a bid to understand his point of view. They talk, both listening to each other's feelings about the position of the now-wretched sofa. In that moment, something shifts. They realise there is another option that neither had thought of: they can move the table to make more room and two chairs that aren't being used at all can go. Because they had got locked into 'my way or your way' thinking, they couldn't see the other's perspective. Therefore, no alternative possibilities were evident to them until they could really listen to and take in the other's truth. The Chesterfield is now in a glorious new position which works much better than either of the other options. Jake and Daphne have the satisfaction of being in the win-win state, found through acknowledging there is a third way. They engaged the perspective of the third body.

How to grow and nourish the third body

Not assuming you 'know' your partner

It is natural for the human mind to try to make sense of why our partner thinks or behaves in a certain way, or how they came to have certain traits. There are many theories of human and psychological development which we can seize on to pathologise our partner, using labels such as 'narcissistic' or 'paranoid'. On one hand, it depersonalises their behaviour to us, making them the one with the problem, as if we have nothing to do with it. On the other hand, it can come across as judgemental and only serves to raise the defences of the other.

Our minds create internal working models of the world and people around us. Over time, this leads to a process known as automisation, whereby attention is transferred from the sensory experience of the person in front of us to the internalised mental abstraction in our minds. This can mean we fail to experience the person at all and only refer to our internalised version of them. Our internal working models and mental abstractions develop and evolve over years of contact with different people. We then add these thought constructions to our experience of people in what is known in psychological language as projection and transference. This leads to misrepresentations and misunderstanding of our partner. For example, if a previous partner has had anger issues, we might assume that our partner is angry with us because they have been distant or a bit uncommunicative, when perhaps instead they have just been busy, tired or preoccupied.

Ultimately, labelling your partner makes them into an 'other'. It separates them and flattens them out into a two-dimensional cut-out, stifling the potential for imagination and play. It is important to remember that you cannot know and do not know your partner completely. It is the unknown-ness of the other that opens the door to mystery and creativity.

The act of projection can be so powerful at times that the person in front of us can actually become that person that our internalised mental abstraction has decided they are. This happens because the projection we make on to them is so strong that the other behaves in ways that are consistent with our internal working model.

Not trying to fix the problem

It's very common for people to want to transform an obdurate partner into an obliging one. And sometimes when a relationship is in trouble, people make choices based on the belief they can fix some defect or another that they have identified in their unfortunate partner. Alas, this rarely works. Focusing on the things you don't like in your partner and trying to change them will most likely have the opposite effect, reinforcing the behaviour you were complaining about in the first place. When we accept our partner for who they are, the process of change often begins. And when we accept ourselves, the same is also true.

Rainer Maria Rilke aptly draws on this paradox of change by reversing the command 'You must change your life!' into 'You must live your changes!' When we believe that we must change our life, we can become paralysed by fear at the immensity of the task. But when we accept that changes in life are inevitable, we are challenged to be mobile and fluid and live those changes instead. When you accept a problem, you can then start working out ways to deal with it. Living your changes is action- and process-orientated and leads to personal change too, whereas the directive to change your life has to start with thinking, which can lead to circular diversions and inactivity.

We need to experience a situation fully before we can overcome it. Feelings, when experienced fully, can transform and dissipate. But feelings that are repressed and not experienced can give rise to obsessive thinking or unhealthy acting out. The fact is, you can't leave a place until you've arrived. When feelings are experienced, when you go to that place, then you can leave. If we allow ourselves to experience emotions and situations before trying to fix problems, we can then resolve them more quickly.

To help identify and experience feelings, it can be useful to map the psychological, emotional and behavioural functions to different areas of the body: thinking to the head, feelings to the heart and behaviour to the action-oriented limbs. To experience feelings, we need to shift awareness to the centre cavity of the body and the regulatory organ of the heart. Feelings transcend thought and action and help us to live more fully. Change can happen if you stay centred in your feelings, tolerate not knowing and hold the dilemma of both/and paradox.

'Not knowing' and allowing generates empathy

Expectations of our partner drawn from our internal models can set us up for disappointment. We can either bring each other down by projecting a negative view of our partner on to them, or we can build them up by seeing the best in them. When we are in a state of 'not knowing', when we have an open mind and suspend all our ideas and assumptions about them, then we have the ability to be curious about our partner. To obtain a state of 'not knowing' is to reverse the projection of our internalised mental abstraction of them. The aim is to lay aside our projections, prejudices and personal egotistical ideals of right and wrong and instead become aware of the experiences of the other person in our mind and sensations. We can then get a 'sense' of the 'I' in our partner that is thinking, that has aspirations, dreams and desires. We can become receptive through a reversal of our own will to welcome in our partner. Our own feelings can be a sense organ for the feelings of another. And our minds can be a receiver of another's thoughts. They feel us feeling them; mind affects mind. Two people can be in sync by allowing the space of 'not knowing' to pulse and transmit between them as the third body.

We limit and contain our partner by judging and theorising about them, by putting them in a box, which is common for couples to do. But instead, we need to allow them to speak for and be themselves by holding back our own ego nature. This requires us to enter a mode of receptiveness through a reversal of our habitual will to know and label.

Surrendering the known invites the third body

Partners can have conflicting ideals and values in areas of life such as scientific outlook, spirituality, philosophy, religion, politics or culture. Even when partners are aligned on some of the above, there are then many different ways of interpreting the circumstances and events of life as they happen, which can cause division and strife. If we are to find peace in the world between neighbours, communities and nations, we must surely first find it in our intimate relationships. It is with our significant others where it shows up most and first offers us the challenge to lay aside our own egos.

NAVIN AND ASHA

Navin and Asha thought they were incompatible because they had different spiritual beliefs. But after analysing this, they realised that the problem was not what they believed but how Navin was discounting Asha's views. In their discussions, which seemed to continually cycle back to this theme in so many ways, Navin was saying he was right and Asha was wrong. The way they saw the world was actually not that different; it was the way that Navin was so dogmatic in his views that was causing the division. Asha was interested in Navin's beliefs but was shut down and pushed away by his arrogance. As they began to unwrap some of the dynamics between them, Navin could understand how Asha's outlook had equal validity to his own. They were just different. Asha could see that it was Navin's opinionated stance that was so off-putting and was creating the incompatibility, not the views themselves. Navin could see that Asha and he could live in harmony if he stepped aside and let her in.

Of course, this is not a one-off event, but presents as an opportunity in each moment of living in a relationship. Navin and Asha, and others like them, are constantly faced with the choice: me, you or us. Accepting the differences and including them, not rejecting them, is the answer. Realising that loving our partner means we have to let go of our own ego and see the world from another's perspective.

In the times when we don't see the beauty in each other, we can call back the memory of who they really are, even if now we don't see it. That is what we can do for each other in relationships: remember the person your beloved partner can be and who you saw them to be when you met. In strife, this gets obscured.

Relationships are about the growth of each individual. We meet things in each other which we need for our own growth. Growth can be painful. It's easier to blame and vilify our partner instead of going through the humiliation and pain of growing. Each of you holds one part of the big, mysterious truth of existence.

Our story

A few years into our marriage, we were keen to have a baby. We were married, had moved into our first flat together and the time was right. That made passion all the more electric, with the anticipation of creating life and starting a family.

Many months later, with no pregnancy happening, we started to worry. We were told it was normal to take a year to conceive, though our friends seemed to be conceiving in nanoseconds. We were healthy and seemed to be doing what it takes. We had a hunch something was wrong. We started being logistical – we timed sex to coincide with the right day of ovulation, with the optimum sperm ejaculate. Sex got methodical, calculated and serious. We were given a plethora of advice from all different directions; it was dizzying and brought our most sacred, private activity into the public realm. Sex became a project that we were failing at, an agenda that we couldn't fulfil. It caused stress and anguish. We'd argue over the details of following the piece of advice we were trying at the time, one of us thinking the other wasn't doing it properly, that it was their fault for not adhering to the method precisely. We tried everything, as our sense of ourselves as a healthy, virile couple was collapsing. We went through many investigations and tests and increasingly complex treatments. We passed many milestones of thinking 'we're not a couple who would do that' to being a couple who was.

Eventually, two long years later, following fertility treatment in a clinical setting, we had good news. Double celebrations and a little trepidation – it was twins. Two in one, a ready-made family. We were overjoyed. Our bond strengthened as we got ready for the babies to come, and our transition to parenthood. We prepared all we could for the arrival of twins, reading the parenting books and getting our small flat kitted out with all the equipment and myriad of essentials that babies need.

Up to their births, they had been perfectly healthy, both a good weight, and everything looked rosy. The birth of the first baby went fine; for the second baby, it went gradually and badly wrong, like a slow-motion movie. A whole series of misjudgements and mistakes occurred, including errors of judgement by one of the midwives, that led to a horrific medical negligence situation and one of the babies being deprived of oxygen for too long. His brain damage kept him on the brink of death for a torturous nine months of intensive care, first in the hospital and then at home. The complexity of caring for twins when one is a lively, thriving baby and the other an acutely unwell baby stretched us in profoundly painful ways.

We grieved in very different ways for his death, for the subsequent miscarriages, for our lost dreams of a bigger family. We had bereavement therapy at the Tavistock Clinic, which helped us unpack the hideous torment and tolerate the different ways we grieved. We blamed each other: if only you had . . . if only you hadn't . . . if only you were different . . . Inevitably, the unspoken 'if only I hadn't married you' was underneath all of them. If I wasn't with you, this wouldn't have happened.

The grief altered us irreversibly; anger and heartbreak became the ground of our third body. The space between us was a tangled mix of emotions that included a huge amount of joy, as our surviving baby lit up our worlds. They were tough times and we had lots of therapy with a skilled and kind therapist. And, as a little family, we held together, learning to feel deeply grateful for what we did have. Our thriving son continued to stride into life in the most beautiful way. He is everything we ever wanted in a child; we feel blessed with the family we have.

Exercises

How do you experience your third body, the space between you? Each take a piece of paper and come up with some names for it. Sometimes, it might be a difficult space and other times, a pleasant one, so the names might reflect all of its flavours and nuances. Ensure you come up with a balance of names that reflects the space in all its different states.

Daily Temperature Reading

A 'daily temperature reading' gives a gauge of the climate of the connection. It can also help to repair, to build interest in each other and warm the environment. We were introduced to this exercise early on in our relationship, in one of the first relationship workshops we attended. It is a communication tool that has been, and still is, a linchpin, invaluable to us over the 20-plus years of being together. Even through difficult patches, when we could barely talk to each other at all, we were still able (not always, but often), to do a 'DTR'. We've managed to do DTRs when we were in such low places that it was the only way we could communicate with any civility. At other times, it has been the icing on the cake, helping to strengthen our relationship and provide a structure for a deepening of conversation. The late psychotherapist Stanley Keleman defined loving someone as 'having the courage to show them whom we really are'. However we're getting on, well or badly, it's one of our core techniques to help us reconnect.

Our exercise is based on the original devised by Virginia Satir and has been used extensively by couples, families, friendships and friendship groups, in workplaces and neighbourhoods.

Set aside 20 minutes if you can. If you don't have that long, it's still possible: when we've been pushed for time we have set a clock, allowing two minutes for each of the five steps. If you have more time there is the luxury of being able to relax into the process – sometimes we have spent the whole evening, or a long car journey, thoroughly unpacking each step. If your relationship is in a fragile state, be patient with each other while you're learning the DTR. As you practise, you will develop speaking and listening skills as well as kindness and compassion. Begin with smaller issues to give yourselves a chance to get to know the process and be comfortable with it.

The Five Steps of the Daily Temperature Reading:
1. Appreciations

You've already been practising this first step of the daily temperature reading as a stand-alone exercise from the beginning of this book. Now you can add the other four steps.

Think of things you each appreciate that the other person did. Showing gratitude enhances life and wellbeing. If you tend to have a negative bias, hold grudges or feel unacknowledged, this can help to shift that. Loving someone is having the courage to show them who we really are.

I appreciate how you . . .

I really liked it when you . . .

Thank you for . . .

Give yourself a moment to fully take in the appreciations, then thank your partner.

2. New information

Think of something you haven't shared with your partner before. Being fluid and spontaneous in your communication helps to keep the channels open between you.

I want to tell you about . . .

Something new that happened is . . .

There was a change in . . .

This can range from small things in your life to big disclosures. It's good to have a few statements which begin with 'I' and make some personal disclosures to your partner.

3. Puzzles

What are you curious about in relation to your partner? What's on your mind? What issues are you struggling with? Being interested in your partner is essential. This is not a cloak for a complaint, it's a place for genuine questions.

Why did you . . .

I'm curious about . . .

I wonder why . . .

This helps to get you on track with your partner's life. Knowing the questions to ask indicates how much you already know about what is happening for them.

4. Requests for change

Name a behaviour you didn't like, say how you felt about it, explain the story that you tell yourself about the behaviour and describe what you would prefer instead. Offer this as a gift, revealing something about yourself, rather than a criticism or in anger.

When you . . . (describe the behaviour in an objective, non-judgemental way)

I felt . . . (describe the feelings you felt in a non-blaming way)

The story I told myself was . . . (tell your partner what you thought to yourself about the behaviour)

I would prefer it if you . . . (say calmly what you would prefer your partner to do instead)

This request for change is given in good faith. The person giving the request for change is disclosing their inner world of personal feelings and thoughts, explaining how a change could help them live a more joyful life. It is important that the partner receiving the request for change does not defend or dispute what they hear but instead just thanks them for it.

5. Wishes, hopes, dreams

Share any aspirations, anticipations, longings, desires, ideas or daydreams. It can be for yourself, your partner, for the relationship or a friend or relative – anybody who is on your mind. It can be for today, tomorrow or next year. It could be something small – such as, 'I hope we find time to make love this weekend' or 'my wish is that my father gets better soon' – or big and out of the box – such as, 'I dream of us starting a family' or 'I hope we move house in the next five years'. You're putting something out there for your partner to hear. You are seeding an idea. These wishes, hopes and dreams help to strengthen your bond as a couple because they show that you hold your partner, their life and the people important to them in your mind. And wishes sometimes come true!

I hope that . . .

I would love to . . .

My dream is . . . .

Putting out a positive message has power as it lingers in the mind and focuses on a joyous outcome.

8

Sense of Self in Relationships

'The Growth of the Self requires opposite tendencies:
Differentiation and Integration.'
– MIHALY CSIKSZENTMIHALYI, FLOW

Inter-dependence and healthy relationships

Healthy relationships are found where partners can function independently and inter-dependently. Co-dependent relationships, on the other hand, are formed of necessity and neediness. You have to stay because you cannot manage on your own. In contrast, a voluntary relationship is where two independent adults choose to love each other and stay together because they want to. They know that they are making a choice to stay together, and that choice can be continually renewed. These partners take responsibility for the relationship they have created and continue to create between them. They do things for the good of the relationship, to nourish and grow the third body. They acknowledge there is a field between them that thrives on loving gestures from both of them and from which they both benefit in equal measure.

Relationships need to keep moving and growing to be healthy, or they go in the opposite direction towards stagnation, dysfunction and eventual death. But relationships cannot grow without the individuals in them committing to their individual growth. We meet things in each other which we need for our own growth. Growth can be painful. It's easier to blame and vilify our partner instead of going through the humiliation and pain of growing. Although we may appear to be constantly faced with choosing between me or you – between my needs and yours, and between my desires and yours – the third body perspective shows that we can include both. In fact, for real growth to occur, we need to include both. For the third body to flourish, we have to show our most intimate selves to our partner, and to do that, we have to be able to find our own sense of who we are as separate beings – to differentiate from our partners – within the relationship.

Learning to separate

The first few months and years of life are in a mutual bond with the 'mother', biological or otherwise. The infant survives through the nurturing of a carer to provide food, warmth and love. The carer helps the child process their emotions by empathising with them; this support helps the child to develop a vibrant interior life. As the child grows, they learn what it means to be an individual self, separate from the carer. Ruptures inevitably occur, due to the stress and pressure of family life, work life, financial worries, illnesses, separations – which can feel like abandonment to the child.

Over the years, friendships and family help us to tolerate the existential awareness of solitariness and manage the pain of separation. When we arrive at adulthood, we can feel exhilarated, free and independent, but the memory of symbiotic bonding is never far away and, at times, the loneliness of existence in an individual body is all too real. This yearning motivates us to look for others with whom we can share experiences and a sense of togetherness.

At the beginning stages of relationship, both people are trying to be their best, to live up to what their partner sees in them. This is the 'we' stage, when the couple merge and everything feels shared. But often, down the line, disappointment hits – 'Have I made a terrible mistake?' At this point, the will to merge becomes the will to differentiate and become separate again. We start to see our partners in a different way, as if they really are separate and sometimes foreign to us.

Another typical dynamic that helps to make a relationship feel secure is borrowed functioning. This is where a couple find a perfect fit because one person fulfils functions that the other cannot perform so well or does not possess at all in themselves. We all have strengths and weakness and so this complementarity is something that brings both partners closer together. It could be an aspect of character, or a particular aptitude or skill.

But after a period of time, one partner may find it too much work to function for the other. We get tired and a little bored of always doing this same thing for our partner that they don't do for themselves. We want them to start to stand on their own two feet and not rely on us anymore. We discover that the experience of security, of merging with our lover, can become claustrophobic and the magnetic energy that propelled us together reverses to push us apart. As relationships mature, each partner must eventually 'give back' certain functions and capacities that they borrowed.

JO AND PETER

Jo and Peter had many happy dates at jazz concerts. Their mutual appreciation of jazz brought them together. Years later, Jo says she isn't so keen and really would rather hear the Royal Philharmonic Orchestra. Peter is shocked and rather hurt; he believed that she really loved jazz. He feels vulnerable and begins to wonder who Jo is. He has to reconfigure his idea of her. He says, 'But I married a jazz fan. We're a jazz couple, we have jazz friends.' Jo had felt her waning interest in jazz for a while, but hadn't liked to say, for fear of letting Peter down and hurting his feelings. She had become more interested in jazz when she and Peter got together, she enjoyed it for the dates they had, but now she misses a broader musical variety.

When Jo states her preferences, she is doing what is called differentiating from Peter. Jo knows she needs to reclaim a lost part of herself and by saying what she wants, she is defining herself as different to Peter. This differentiation will help their relationship become stronger in the long run.

The forces of differentiation and merging

A healthy relationship has a balance of differentiation and merging. Differentiation is moving away from your partner and defining yourself as separate to them. It is a shift away from similarity and towards uniqueness, standing on your own two feet, and feeling whole and independent as an individual. Integration or merging is a process of moving towards sameness with your partner. Both these forces must work together for a relationship to evolve and grow and to remain alive and vibrant.

Some couples tend more to differentiation and others towards merging. Those who habitually differentiate strive for independence, value autonomy and fear dependency. Those who habitually merge strive for unity, oneness, safety and similarity with the other, and fear being different. Yet there is a balance to be struck between them, which is healthy inter-dependence, and is required for growth in relationships. This can be described as the ability to be comfortable in merging while also allowing difference between you. It is the ability to admit to needing and being needed in your relationship while taking responsibility for yourself as a differentiated adult. The movement from one stance to another is the process that builds trust and resilience in a relationship. The ability to move fluidly from 'I' to 'we' and back to 'I' gives us perspective on ourselves and each other. If we get stuck in either position, we limit the potential for the relationship.

The same two movements happen inside us. Moving away is differentiating, stepping back and seeing the distinctions between the many parts of ourselves, the parts we like and the parts we don't like so much, and being able to redefine the self in any given moment. The process of differentiation within the self enables us to maintain self-awareness, while merging allows us to integrate those parts of the self that we have disowned because they are too difficult or painful. This is how we can become more self-aware and fully integrated human beings. The more integrated we are, the more space there is for the third body to flourish.

Being a differentiated adult creates more aliveness in the relationship because you can speak your truth and mind. You honour yourself and take responsibility for your needs and your views. You accept that your partner may or may not agree with or approve of you. It takes courage to be different to your partner. Especially at the beginning of a relationship, when there is a magnetic pull to merge and a momentum towards sameness. You can be together but on your own two feet. You can reflect attributes that you have borrowed from your partner. We grow through the continual process of merging and differentiating.

The extreme of the magnetic poles of togetherness and aloneness is felt strongly at the beginning of a love relationship. We cannot move towards someone without moving away from someone or something else. It is an act of courage to join consciously with someone else, to establish a relationship that may or may not be sanctioned by our family, friends, religion or community. Love provides the momentum to do that.

Too much or not enough differentiation

Problems can arise when there are no clear boundaries between you and your partner in the relationship, and therefore not enough 'moving away' and differentiating, or when the boundaries are too rigid and there is not enough 'moving towards'. In Chapter Four, we used the analogy of the octopus and the turtle for two styles of attachment, of moving towards and moving away from our intimate connections. The octopus, with its tentacles, seeks out and moves towards connection. The turtle is self-sufficient and prone to retreating into its hard shell; it is resourceful and independent and likes to restore and recharge in solitude or solitary pursuits.

When our partner becomes more important to us than we are to ourselves, when we prioritise their needs over ours, we have to find ways to differentiate. The feelings of being separate and alone can be so unbearable that we seek symbiotic union, to lose ourselves in merging with someone or something. We form a kind of co-dependent relationship, where the fusion of the relationship subsumes the self. Addictions can also be a substitute for the long-lost feeling of the original union.

On the other hand, if there are always other things to attend to besides our partner, when we prioritise every-thing in our life over the relationship, then we need to find ways to move towards.

FRED AND ANNA

Fred is a financially prosperous 65-year-old. He'd always hoped to retire at the top of his career and finally spend quality time with his wife, Anna. However, while he has been very successful at work, Anna has left him. After 20 years of feeling lonely in the marriage, increasingly unable to attract his attention and exhausted by trying, she has now petitioned for a divorce.

Fred has a turtle attachment style. He was so wrapped up in his own life that he had no idea she was so unhappy until it was too late. He worked all hours, even taking his laptop on holidays. Now Fred is sorely regretting taking her for granted, undervaluing the relationship and prioritising work. He had the comfortable lifestyle he had worked so hard to earn, yet, facing his retirement alone, is bewildered about how to build a relationship.

We create ourselves together

The synthesis of information from external sources and from our own interior experience forms our vision of reality. Our five senses allow us to absorb millions of pieces of sensory data and fit them into our internal working models of the world, which have been formed from our beliefs and assumptions of how things should be. When we are faced with a different reality to our own in our partner, who sees things otherwise to us, we have a choice of moving towards that reality and trying to understand it or of moving away from it and staying in our own 'fishbowl'.

The contradictory movements towards or away from each other are how we construct ourselves. We are making and being made together. In a conversation, we move towards the other's thought processes to join, understand and empathise with them. We move inwards, towards our thoughts and feelings, and away from theirs, so we can take a moment to formulate a response. Between the polarities of fusion and separation, there is a space created, which is where the third body exists. This is a healing space.

When we get together with someone with whom we resonate, we know we have a reason to choose them. We look for someone who will understand our reality, break through into our world and relieve our isolation, separation or loneliness. It is immensely rewarding when we take the risk to express the truth of our inner landscape and feel validated. We receive the connection we crave. The simple act of making contact with somebody important to us is valuable in itself. When we connect in a way that acknowledges us and feels safe, there is room for us, and we know we are respected and loved. But when things don't go so well, it isn't safe for us to be honest, we don't feel met or our partner is controlling us in a way that deprives us of our freedom, we have to make a choice. Do we take the risk and express how we feel, even though they may not like it? It might feel challenging to go against your partner and describe your experience, but when you do, you change who you are. In contact, we simultaneously reveal ourselves and also create ourselves at that place where I meet you, or I meet the world. I am changed by who and what I encounter. We change each other. We get together with someone with the idea that we know who they are, yet their mystery continues as we continue to get to know them throughout our relationship. Even established couples are always learning new things about one another. That's the exciting part.

JANICE AND DIEGO

It is no coincidence that Janice and Diego both carry trauma from their childhood. They resonate with each other's wounds below the level of awareness. Janice is similar in some ways to Diego's mother and him to her father. As with many 'good matches', this initially provided the opportunity for healing the wounds from those early parental relationships.

Diego never had enough attention from his mother, who was often preoccupied with her thoughts and aloof. After his father left when he was young, he and his younger sister were often looked after by au pairs, while his mother followed her career goals. Diego was an anxious child. He remembers looking out of the window and waiting for his mother to come home, fearful she had been in a car crash and would never return. This fear of abandonment is still with him today and is something he is healing gradually in his relationship with Janice.

Janice grew up in a tense household with an angry and aggressive father who would shout and throw things around the room. She didn't feel loved by him and became hostile, particularly when she received negative attention and criticism from him for not doing things well enough. Janice's father frightened her and her mother. Janice observed how her mother managed her father by shutting down and being quiet. It was a strategy that worked. Without the fuel of her mother arguing back, her angry father would eventually retreat.

Diego is fastidiously on time for everything. However, Janice is not. Diego ends up waiting for Janice much of the time. This reminds him of the anxious times he waited for his mother when he was five, worrying she had died in a car accident. His response to these vulnerable feelings is to get angry with Janice when she eventually turns up. Janice is an easy-going soul who doesn't quite see the fuss. She often waits for her friends and is happy to watch the world go by, read her book or check her phone. But Diego can't do that. His anxious mind keeps telling him that he is 'waiting, waiting, waiting'. When Janice arrives, he criticises her, accusing her of being selfish and unreasonable for keeping him waiting. Janice begins to feel uncomfortable. Images of her father thrashing the air with his fists and shouting come flooding back. She tries to reason with Diego but he gets more wound up. She says to herself, 'Oh, here we go again.' She reads the situation as hopeless and shuts down to protect herself, the way she learned from her mother all those years ago.

Now things take another turn. When Janice shuts down and moves away emotionally from Diego, this leaves him feeling even more abandoned. This hurt exacerbates his anger, and he gets even more agitated and annoyed with Janice, trying to get some sympathy and understanding from her. Now the spiral is plummeting downwards. The angrier he gets, the more Janice withdraws and shuts down. The more she distances, the angrier he gets. They are as far apart as ever and both are hurting.

In therapy, they see how they respond to each other from old constructs, stemming from when they were vulnerable children. Past experiences and their emotional responses to them are fuelling how they see and react to each other in the present. Once this is understood and felt internally, *each of them begins the process of devising new scripts aimed at soothing the distressed inner child. They must move their attention towards, their painful experience and self-soothe. This calming is often challenging, and it is far easier to blame the other. But when they can self-soothe and look after their own inner child, they can begin to do that for each other, getting underneath the other's experience, understanding it and healing each other.*

What is also at stake is the opportunity for more intimacy between them. Moving towards their internal sensations and feelings is a move towards more intimacy and connection with themselves. The quality of a relationship with another depends on the quality of the relationship with yourself. And vice-versa. They talk about their feelings and how they misattributed their cause to each other, which starts to build trust, necessary for intimacy. Janice also realises how she lets her boundaries slip, causing her to be late. She hasn't been good at being precise with herself and committing to being on time. When Janice can take in how important it is for Diego, she shifts significantly in transforming her attitude to this. She practises grounding herself – a simple meditation of giving attention to the ground under her and her body's contact with the environment helps her clear her mind. Diego acknowledges how his rigidity adds to his anxiety. He practises giving attention to his breathing, and finds it helps him calm down and gives him more of a sense of himself. When he relaxes, softens his body and finds compassion for himself, he finds more composure in his emotions with Janice.

The psychoanalyst Donald Winnicott sums up the great paradox of the human condition when he says, 'It's a joy to be hidden and a disaster not to be found.' We want to hide sometimes, but we also want someone to find us. Being hidden and found is part of the process of being separate from our partner but then feeling the need to be connected again. It oscillates from one pole to the other, and relationships are created through this movement towards and away. Love is searching for and finding each other. We need someone to discover us to understand who we are. We see each other through taking each other in and understanding. When we feel understood, we feel as if we have been found. This contact gives us self-definition and validation.

'Us' vs 'I'

What it feels like to be me

Living life with ourselves is challenging enough. And we often forget that our starting point for making relationships is this primary relationship with ourselves. We form ourselves through the interactions we have with people all lifelong. We have many facets to the self and modes of behaviour, which we draw on to meet the needs of specific situations. To complicate things further, we each have interactions between our thoughts, feelings and impulses which, at times of stress or overwhelm, can get out of balance. At such times, we may feel unhappy or dissatisfied with ourselves, causing problems in our relationship with our partner. And equally, a problematic relationship with our partner can negatively impact an otherwise good sense of who we are.

Being satisfied in your relationship often depends on how aspects of you interact with thoughts, feelings and bodily sensations generated within you when you are with your partner. Facing things in yourself means becoming aware of, making contact with and acknowledging all the parts of you, even those you may not like.

When we turn our attention to how we are feeling physically it can unlock our feelings, thoughts and sensations, allowing us to be conscious of them. From this place of full bodily awareness, we have more freedom to choose how we want to act. It is so habitual for many of us to go along with whatever is happening and automatically adapt ourselves to it.

Most of us want to 'cherry pick' all the positive feelings and ignore the difficult ones. A way of doing this might be by drinking, overeating or a screen addiction; or we become a workaholic or some other compulsion that might be successful in distracting us from uncomfortable sensations, at least for a while. Feelings in our body impact us one way or another, whether we are aware of them or not. Embodiment is the continually evolving process of merging our awareness with our sensate body, in each present moment. When we are embodied, we are consciously aware of all the sensations and feelings in our bodies. But it isn't a state we arrive at in an immediate way: it is an ongoing practice.

Our bodies are intricately connected with our thoughts, feelings and impulses, yet often there is a splitting off – we are thinking one thing and doing another, or feeling something and making efforts not to show it. We're socialised to do that: it means we can be polite, fit in, stay safe. We get to keep our jobs even when we don't like our boss, or live alongside annoying neighbours, or have Christmas with family that might trigger us. Sometimes we feel detached or have no awareness of our feelings because we have distanced ourselves from our own body. That's why it is important to give extra attention to your connection with bodily sensations. Our bodies reflect physically what we feel internally.

Our playfulness and creativity can come to the fore when we learn to trust our bodies and feelings, and to heed our own wisdom. When we are willing to welcome it all, we free ourselves from the exhaustion of avoidance and open ourselves to the spaciousness of being exactly as we are. When we practise noticing our sensations, we can come more into connection with ourselves and we then have more of our selves available to us. The more our senses are available to us, the easier it becomes to improve the relationship we have with ourselves and others.

What it feels like to be us

A good relationship benefits our health on every level. Somewhere in the middle, between wanting closeness and independence, is a beautiful balance, which we can see metaphorically as the dance. In it, we find the equilibrium, which is exhilarating. We find a way to connect again to ourselves, and to manage the differing needs and desires of yourself, your partner and the relationship as the third body. In moments of stress in the relationship, the pole of being apart can be a haven of retreat. But doing this too much can exacerbate problems between you, leaving you even more divided. For one, the split creates more hurt in the partner who doesn't retreat. The irony is that when we think we are finding refuge in aloneness, we hurt ourselves too, because we miss the comfort of togetherness. We cannot live solely in either of the extreme states.

One of the ways to come back from this place and to connect more deeply with ourselves and our partners is through feeling and being together in our bodies. Through dance, play, touch and sex, we can learn to move between aloneness and togetherness. When we are aware of our own body, and we extend towards a partner who is also present to their own embodied self, there is a felt sense of both merging and differentiation.

Proprioception is the body's ability to sense itself in space. We utilise proprioception when we are co-ordinated and agile – we can move without bumping into things; we can judge distance and maybe even move fluidly without looking. In cases where someone has a prosthetic limb, they can integrate a sense of the limb into their own internal map of the body through the sense of proprioception. In other words, we grow our awareness of the body to include the new limb. Parking a car involves the same ability – we grow the sense of the space we take up to include the size and shape of the car, so that when we park we don't bump into anything. The same thing happens when we emotionally merge with our partner: we extend the sense of our body to include their body. We're walking alongside them and we are one. Unified, combined, we extend the sense of our own body to include theirs. We are more than one person – we become a physical unit. If they have an accident, we might feel it physically in our own body. In these moments, they belong to us and we to them; there isn't a clear delineation of where one body ends and the other begins.

When our partner leaves our side, emotionally and physically, there is a moment of adjustment. It might feel like a slight severance, a sense of something missing, a mini grief. Readjusting means to feel our own feet on the ground, to become whole as an individual again. This is the embodiment of differentiation – regaining a sense of individuation. The sense of proprioception alters to locate just our own body in space and our senses, the things we see, smell, taste, hear and touch, are now just ours, for our pleasure or nourishment. We occupy the space our body is in and inhabit our own physical territory. Merging and differentiating is a process that defines a growthful relationship. The ability to see your partner as a separate individual as well as to join emotionally is important in building intimacy, erotic charge and trust.

Play

Play is often relegated to childhood, its significance under-rated in adulthood. Play is an experience that brings us into contact with our surroundings and expands our creative living. The act of playing enforces and underlies our own sense of agency. It gives us knowledge that we can make things happen, that we have an impact, that we have enough personal power to take action in the world. Play creates a potent space for the third body between us, as both members of the couple connect. The experience of play transforms us and our environments, as we are required to access our inner world of imagination. We enter a zone of phenomenal unpredictability.

Playing is a way that we connect with ourselves; we discover unknown, forgotten or repressed parts of ourselves.

We get to know our ever-changing self, meet our own edges and reinvent ourselves. We get a sense of ourselves as the one who is playing, who simultaneously creates and interacts with the creative zone made by us and others we play with. Mutuality is important here – that is, co-operation and sharing in an equal way. When there is a balance of power, of input, of space taken, of decisions agreed and impulses followed, then there is capacity for limitless experience where we feel truly alive. When we hold ourselves with kindness and compassion, this can be therapeutic. When we enter the zone of play with our partner this extends to our relationship, too.

Maybe you play card games or board games, do a new sport, dance creatively, take on a new persona, role-play, practise spontaneity, play chase, try trampolining – or whatever it is that might sound fun, exciting, novel, experimental and enjoyable to you and your partner. If it is part of some sort of 'improvement plan', then it probably isn't play in the creative sense. We're not talking about something goal focused. If there is a goal in mind (i.e. fitness, losing weight, health improvement or encouraging your partner into a sexy situation), that's something else. The play we're referring to here is play for its own sake, just for fun. It might be that we get fit while we're doing it, or learn something, or somehow improve ourselves, but let that be by-product, not the intention.

When a couple is in harmony, play can come easily. And when two people are in a place of pain or conflict, it is impossible. Playing with a partner also requires that you differentiate from them. If you are merged, it will be difficult to play different roles. Play can also highlight unresolved aspects of a relationship, like the example of Jerome and Veronica on their cycling trip in Chapter Three – they found parts of their relationship that they didn't enjoy. The irony of recreation and time off is that we look forward to it, but they can often highlight difficulties that are being avoided in day-to-day life. Holidays, with all the unpredictability involved, can often be a time of tension and conflict, which need repair in order to make a safe space for play.

Experiencing the third body through dance

In choreographed dance, like tango or ballroom, there are specific techniques which can be crafted, practised and perfected. In improvised dance, the dancer follows their impulses, creating the movement in the moment. The Open Floor movement modality that we work with is improvised; it's not about technique or form, it's about tuning into sensations, emotions and thoughts, and finding ways of expressing that in movement. We learn about ourselves and our patterns, and we can practise new ways of relating.

In one of our couples movement workshops, we explore dancing. Dance is a form of play that can be deeply transformative as well as a lot of fun. The room is full, there is enticing music, our dance floor is a playground to explore relationship dynamics through movement. We invite the dancers to notice their own dance and that of their partner, and then to pan out and give attention to the space between them. We invite them to imagine this space as the third body, and they can tend to this in the same way they can give attention to their body or their partner's body. When they start to do this, a palpable shift happens in the room.

At first, it is subtle, and then quite an electric change of direction: there is a wider variety of movement and creativity as people move in more vibrant and liberated ways. One couple has moved apart, their limbs occupying more space around them, and they are looking at each other with delight. Another couple is slowly sinking to the ground, continuing their dance by moving across the floor with a potent prowess. A third couple, who had seemed quite stuck earlier in the workshop, is changing tempo in unpredictable ways: one of them faster and one of them slows down – the mismatch seems to be enlivening for them.

Through dancing, or playing, we sense, without having to discuss it, that there is a third body between us. We can tend to this space, give it attention, relate to it. It is created by the specific alchemy of the pairing. It is there if we give it attention or not. If this was a person – this third body – we can imagine what they would feel.

When both partners feel energised and supported, the relationship challenges in life become manageable, laden with potential for change. There's a 'thing' happening – a vibe, some contact – and it brings meaning, support and value to life.

Sex

At its best, sex can involve every aspect of the human organism: psychological, neurological, hormonal, physio-logical, emotional, spiritual and playful. Sex as adult play is an important aspect of it. When we talk about sex as play, we are not talking about the kind of play that is bound by rules or that has an objective, like a game of tennis or football.

That would be missing the point because sexual encounters are often already focused on an objective, such as making it a good performance or achieving a great orgasm. The type of play we are talking about here is play for enjoyment and recreation, rather than for any intended purpose. Play, in purest form, is to be present in the zone and in the flow. Sex as play is process-based and takes place in the space between you, where each can unfold their world of desires, imagination and creativity. When sex can be playful in this sense it opens up realms of possibility where the space between you is timeless and can be found and re-found wherever you are and at whatever age.

Though, while being able to play is fun, it can also be challenging, as it requires an ability to express feelings, thoughts and impulses, and to give up control, predetermined ideas and strategies, and instead be open to any outcome. We'll talk more about sex and interdependence in the following chapter.

Our story

We were trying something new. It was a bike trip, cycling the perimeter of the Isle of Wight, the three of us, over a much-anticipated and well-planned few days, staying along the route in pre-booked B&Bs. Booking the accommodation in advance meant some anxiety about getting to the planned evening destination. We hoped our son, aged 12 at the time, was old enough to keep up with us, yet not too old to find us slow.

On the first day, we were in high spirits, off on our adventurous holiday on the beautiful Isle of Wight.

Yet those spirits soon faded as the reality of the hard work up and down the hills set in. The second day, we started out feeling tired and then encountered rain and unexpectedly high winds during bumpy uphill climbs. It was physically uncomfortable and emotionally disappointing. Our son was tired and whingeing, and we had been arguing about something trivial.

On one particular route, midway up a large, windswept hill, with views stretching out, Matt, ahead of the others, stopped, got off his bike and put his bike on the ground. As Sarah and our son got to him, Matt indicated to put our bikes down. Matt, in his ever kind, caring way, said he needed to tell us that he hated this situation and that he hated how we were being with each other. He proposed an exercise for us all to vent our frustration and clear the air. 'Good idea,' said Sarah, who was looking limp and withdrawn. 'I hate this!' shouted Matt into the air above him (though first of all making sure that no one else was around!). He repeated it a few times, putting more energy into it each time. 'I hate this!' 'I hate this!' Then he shouted, 'I won't take it!' 'I won't take it!' 'I won't take it!' The others looked on in astonishment, as Matt was really getting into it, clenching his fists and stamping his feet on the ground, going red in the face. Then we all got the excitement of it. It was quite ceremonial and very energising. Sarah and our son started to join in, shouting, 'I hate this! I won't take it!', stamping and clenching our fists. We all felt elated by the revelation of authentic expression. Then Matt suddenly changed. He loosened his body, stood up straight and said calmly: 'I will take it.' 'I will take it.' 'I will take it.'

Screaming 'I hate this' and 'I won't take it' might sound disruptive, but the gradual building stress had already caused the disruption. Instead of trying to look on the bright side, we surrendered to the loathsome feelings we'd been trying to avoid. We gave up trying to be sunny and surrendered to the clouds. What we were doing was expressing our 'no' to our exhausting and tedious experiences.

The 'no' is expressed fully using the body and muscle tension in contraction and release cycles. Once it has been fully expressed, the 'yes' can come. We can accept what is happening. We might not like it, but we accept it. This unusual intervention was, paradoxically, part of the repair. It used harsh language in a way that was connecting rather than disconnecting and saying the unsayable, uttering taboo words in a bid for connection with each other. Matt set up the situation carefully, giving us warning as to what he wanted to do and waited for consent. He had been on a self-development workshop led by the Kairos Foundation, and it is a process that he adapted from their programme.

Having a witness can help sear a view into our minds. An external perspective is like a mirror. On that day on the Isle of Wight, a person was walking their dog some distance away, out of earshot. If the wind had carried our words, they would have heard us. We could see the theatricality, the almost pitiful sight of these three tired cyclists amid a challenging few days. We laughed at the strangeness of how this scene would appear. Humour helped the repair; we felt connected in our laughter. The paradox is that in expressing 'no', we were able to feel love for each other and the situation.

Exercises

The Bossy Massage

This exercise comes from Betty Martin, who developed the 'Wheel of Consent' work. We find this exercise so liberating – as a receiver, we have the luxury of giving ourselves attention, and as a server, to be in service. We trained with Betty Martin and now offer aspects of her work in our workshops. When we teach others Bossy Massage, it invariably takes the 'receivers' some time to digest the fact that this is for them to take as much time as they need to listen into what they might want. Nothing will happen until they say so and it will only happen in the way they ask. It doesn't work to say 'give me a back massage' as the instructions have to be precise and specific: 'rub my shoulders with your hands and' move your fingers around the bones at the top of my spine'. At first, it can seem like an effort to ascertain what we might want. Then, in time, an extraordinary liberation comes from the simple art of listening to impulses and being true to them.

- This is for two people; decide on your roles, a receiver and a server.

- Put on a timer for 20–30 minutes. A time boundary is important to hold the session with clarity.

- The receiver gets comfy as you might for a massage, lying down or sitting in a chair – whatever you want. You can change positions at any time. Clothes on is fine. Make sure you're warm enough, for example, with a blanket over you.

- This is not to be the time to succumb to the reverie of

a body massage; it's an experiment in asking for what you want.

- So the receiver takes time to listen in with themselves and how they would like the server to touch them.

- The receiver tells the server how they would like to be touched. If the server is comfortable to do so, they do it for five or ten seconds. You don't need to time it with a stopwatch; it's an approximate yet purposefully short time to minimise the risk of the receiver accepting anything other than precisely what they want. It could be the duration of three or five breaths. The server won't do anything during that time except exactly what the receiver asked. If it is something the server isn't comfortable with, they negotiate. I.e. 'Instead of putting my hands on the front of your face, I can rest a hand on your forehead.'

- If the receiver doesn't know what to ask for, the receiver rests and waits. The server will wait too.

- As they perform each touch, the server checks 'Like this?' 'Is that the spot?' to get confirmation that they're doing what the receiver actually wants. The receiver can guide, 'I want that again, but more pressure on the left hand.' Amazingly, sometimes a very slight difference in the touch is what we want.

The Bossy Massage is a powerful experiment in what happens when you are entirely confident that you are in control of what is happening to you. The structure is intentionally precise, which prevents the receiver from tolerating or enduring it.

The receiver is active, directing the server. The server is passive, doing what the receiver asks for and nothing else.

People often don't know what they want; they are used to going along with what is already happening or what someone else suggests. The intention here is to slow down enough to notice what you want and find out how it is to be absolutely in charge of how you are touched, moment by moment. You trust that enough to value it and have the confidence to choose and ask for it.

The receiver is in contact with themselves and their wants and gets immediate responsive feedback. A Bossy Massage encourages asking directly, in a straightforward order. For some people, this is near impossible. First, they might say, 'you could do this', or 'would you please do that?'. A step further is to drop the 'you could' or 'please' and say 'will you do such-and-such?'. It can feel vulnerable to request 'will you' and 'I want'. And it is often challenging for people to give a direct command – 'put your hands on my knees' or 'lean your left shoulder into my right shoulder blade' – without any filler or preamble.

The server can notice their reaction; they might get impatient or nervous about getting it right, or they might make assumptions about how they interpret the directions. The server, often, is serving by doing less. They are not leading, but following, which can be bewildering for many. It is not about the quality of their creativity or innovation; they need to put that aside and focus on the receiver. If nothing much seems to be happening, trust that there is probably more going on internally for the receiver as they check in with themselves about how they want to be touched.

9

Sex and Desire in Long-term Relationships

The challenges of sex in a long-term relationship

One of the recurring questions we hear from couples in intimate relationships is this: can a long-term relationship sustain a vibrant sexual, emotional and loving connection? Like any activity you enjoy and do repeatedly over time, sometimes sex is amazing, other times neutral and occasionally it might be dull. There's a myth that everyone else is having amazing sex, and having it regularly. We see it in films, or maybe porn, implied in advertising. In reality, no one has great sex all the time. A normal, healthy, happy relationship will have unpredictable fluctuations. Studies differ but they generally show that couples report that about a quarter of the time sex is fantastic, half the time it's mediocre and the rest of the time it's dull, disappointing or downright disastrous. Research also shows that between a quarter and a third of adults have sex in any given week. So, that leaves approximately three-quarters to two-thirds of adults who are not having weekly sex. Yet half of adults report they would like to have more.

Inconsistent satisfaction is inevitable, unavoidable and all part of being human. We find something that works, try it for a while and get really good at it in all its variations. Then the novelty wears off and what was creative and innovative becomes routine, predictable and boring. The stereotype of sex in stable relationships is that it is dull, mundane and boring, and that only in new relationships or affairs do risqué activities bring excitement. But anything becomes boring if we stop exploring.

Familiarity and certainty are the enemies of eroticism

Eroticism thrives between the polarities of familiarity and novelty, certainty and uncertainty, excitement and security. We want certainty to feel safe and uncertainty to feel excited. In this area of greys, between the poles of black and white, lies the greatest potential for eroticism, when there is uncertainty and wishing, exploration and tentativeness. The extreme ends of each pole do not provide the answer. Certainty does not produce excitement or variety but produces boredom. All-out uncertainty brings excitement, but the potential for deeper bonding, which is important for the relationship to grow, is absent. Both poles are static and immobile in their own way. The middle ground, where two habitats meet, is fertile, like the banks of the river or the hedges between fields.

Being together and bonded offers more certainty. We look for certainty in life – an anchor around which to build a family, for instance, or to purchase a property, or plan activities. Certainty allows us to imagine into the future. Our human capacity for visualisation creates new worlds towards which we can strive. Finding a partner might be your aim if you are single. You might be propelled by the thought of loving and sharing your life with someone else, raising children together or going on a road trip.

Yet the beckoning finger of freedom can lure us away from a life of certainty. When we believe our life is too mapped out, we can yearn for uncertainty, which offers us excitement and romance. During courtship and dating, it is this uncertainty which is so alluring. Will they accept me? Like me? Have sex with me? Is this person 'the One'? Will this work out or not? Will I like them? Will they live up to my dreams? Will they fit into my vision? Share my values? In contrast, a life of certainty can feel rather stultifying and stale.

Keeping sex and desire alive in a long-term relationship can be a challenge because familiarity and certainty are the enemies of eroticism. The sexologist Jack Morin, in his book *The Erotic Mind*, introduces the erotic equation: attraction + obstacles = excitement. It is often said that security kills sex. Elicit affairs feel so exciting because there is no security. There is an attraction and the obstacle of maintaining a dual life, the uncertainty of being found out, or of one of you ending it.

EDUARDO AND VALENTINA

Eduardo and Valentina both work full-time and between them must also manage their children. Eduardo's gaze is turned inwards towards vivid pictures of the days before their life changed when children came along. He and Valentina are cruising in his classic open-top Alfa Romeo Giulietta with the wind in their hair and the coastal road winding ahead of them. They both feel the vividness and aliveness of life in those days before they started a family. They thrived on the excitement of those days of uncertainty when they were dating. With the stresses of family life, they were stretched and lost the connection between them.

Eduardo moved out and was then able to tell Valentina that he missed alone time with her. His sexual feelings come alive again when he imagines them being together, just the two of them taking to the road. Valentina yearned for support and emotional closeness. Without this she met some of her needs through being a mother to the children. The separation allowed them to get perspective and feel the longing for the other again. They moved back together with a renewed awareness of the importance of making time for fun and adventure in their relationship to keep the emotional connection alive.

Why have sex?

The motivation for sex in a relationship, other than to start a family, is usually to create and maintain an intimate bond with your partner, to feel wanted and loved by them and to enjoy the pleasure and self-satisfaction of a sexual encounter.

If you have spontaneous desire (see Chapter Two), the question 'why have sex?' may never have occurred to you. Because with spontaneous desire it's about satisfying that desire and celebrating the carnal pleasures of life. If you have contextual desire, there is a broader range of reasons to satisfy, to enable the willingness that is required to get into a sexual situation. Sex as relationship bonding is one of the top reasons people with contextual desire feel willing to get into a sexual situation with their partner. Making love is exactly that: it creates a heart connection of tender warmth and affection between you. It's the glue to your relationship. The alchemy that turns a humdrum relationship into one with the sparkle of gold. This can happen in all three of the sexual arousal styles, which are described later in this chapter.

Extending the meaning of sex

Are you a sexy couple or just a couple who has sex? Being a sexy couple is extending the meaning of sex to include areas of contact more usually considered to be non-sexual. If you pass by each other at home, do you stand back to let your partner through or do you savour the chance to brush past each other, taking a moment for a hug or caress? Walking down the street, do you hold hands or have your arms around each other? Watching a film together, do you snuggle up? These incidental chance moments are golden opportunities for non-sexual touch.

Touch is the one sense we cannot thrive without; it is essential to good health. It's a way we maintain connection and communicate non-verbally, and a necessary part of keeping an intimate relationship thriving. We convey our emotional state in subtle, nuanced ways. Non-sexual touch is any touch where neither of you has the intention of it leading to sex. It might be sexy or arouse sexual feelings but it's still just touching for its own sake, like communication, connection or conversation. The well-timed non-sexual touch from our partner can feel just delectable. Soothing and relaxing. Hugs and kisses cause our bodies to release the natural 'feel-good' chemical oxytocin, the natural antidepressant serotonin, and the pleasure neurotransmitter dopamine. Known as the 'love hormone', oxytocin can promote trust and empathy, increasing bonding and reducing stress, anxiety and depression. Our whole nervous system feels good and we feel in harmony with our partner, experiencing a sense of wellbeing. When non-sexual touch is familiar to us, a daily occurrence, we respond warmly. It is reciprocal and respectful. When non-sexual touch is sparing, we can overreact and be jumpy as if we have been violated, or underreact as if nothing happened. When touch is only ever associated with sex or an invitation for sex, rather than simply for pleasure, physical contact brings a whole agenda that can induce tension and expectation.

Getting turned on

Passion and desire

Being turned on is being in an aroused and desirous state. It's when the body and mind are experiencing and inviting pleasure and sensation. We often equate being turned on with sexual passion. When we feel passionate, we are full of energy and longing for connection with someone or something. In this condition, we feel alive and in a state of flow, engaged and attuned to our process. Passion is energy that goes out. When we think of passion as desire, we mean it is the passion to have sexual union in love. It is the will to unite, to bring someone into you. Passionate love is the feeling of self-expansion when you include within yourself the person you desire. Opening to your partner means to offer psychological and emotional access. Honestly revealing your thoughts and feelings, and being transparent and vulnerable, increases sexual attraction and closeness. Bring yourself to an encounter with your partner with openness and curiosity; be prepared to find something new in them. But come with something to offer, something fresh in yourself too.

When we stop being open about ourselves, our partner will feel the closure. And when we stop being curious about our partner, we will feel turned off towards them. We will cease to find anything interesting anymore because we are no longer looking. Sharing with each other psychologically is important in keep the contact open between you. Psychological intimacy has been shown to increase emotional and sexual intimacy. For instance, some couples never share their fantasies because of fear of appearing abnormal. But sharing inner worlds is a major contributor to turning each other on. If this stops happening, boredom can set in. This is the shadow of passion, which also shows up as laziness, opposition and withdrawal.

You may notice a swing in your relationship from passion to laziness. This is normal and part of the cycle of relating, but there is a risk of getting stuck in either of the polarities or of continually oscillating between the two.

The important thing to remember about passion is that it is relative and contextual. When one of you is feeling passionate, the other may respond by receiving or opposing you. If you push forward, the other might pull back; if you pull back, the other can come forward. Passion needs intention, oxygen and aliveness. Having intention is to have the willingness to be engaged in your relationship and with your partner. Planning something new with your partner, an activity together, will help you feel more intimate. All kinds of intimacy are connected: spending time together and developing emotional intimacy can help build closeness and sexual intimacy, too.

What are you passionate about?

What lights your fire? What catches your eye? There's the passion for life itself, the things that get us up in the morning and put a spring in our step. There's the joy of a spring day or the smell of a good cup of coffee. There's birdsong and birthdays and dancing at parties. Do you have a hobby that fires your mojo? Gardening or gaming, singing or swimming, politics or pottery, angling or activism – there are so many ways to feed our passions, to acknowledge our zest for life in all its glories.

There is an endless list of different things people find turn them on sexually. As we change through life, our turn-ons and fantasies change, and they say a lot about us and what we need and yearn for. That's not to say we need to actually create these fantasies into reality – some fantasies are only ever meant to stay in the imagination. Yet, all of this is normal. Most of us think we're a bit weird or kooky – that's all part of the allure.

What turns you off? Most likely something very close to whatever it is that turns you on – our yuck and our yums are often remarkably similar. Sex can be either massively alluring or wholly debasing. Lust and disgust are not far apart. We want to know what others are doing to find out where we fit in. We all want to be normal. But what is normal and what isn't? What we want in the bedroom is often opposite to what we do in life. For example, the business executive making decisions all day may dream of submissive surrender in the bedroom at night.

Sex sells, sex attracts us; nature all around is positively pulsating with it. Humans and many other species could not continue without it. We need sex for procreation. It's alive and exciting. It's that juicy feeling of vibrancy between you when you first get sexy with someone you really desire. It's a whole body experience. When we feel sexy and alive in our body, we feel emotionally close and connected. Sexual arousal is the force that works within each of us, bringing our thoughts, feelings and impulses into joyous harmony. We feel loving and sexy in ourselves and towards each other. It works in the space between us, filling it with an intoxicating energy.

What turns you off?

The paradox in a long-term relationship is that the sex that brought the couple together often turns out to be what splits them up. Division in sex comes in a multitude of forms. What is a turn-on for one is a turn-off for the other. Who is in the mood and who isn't? Who wants it, when and how often? For some it's once a day and for others once a month. Partners pathologise each other, telling the other they're not normal, complaining they are either a sex maniac or frigid; they want it too much or not enough; they're insatiable or unreachable; they're too hot or too cold, or just the wrong temperature at the wrong time. It can become about one person's needs over another.

Other sources of division through sex can be a lack of sexual opportunity and changing feelings about its relevance when a baby comes along; emotional difficulties between partners because of unexpressed thoughts; hurt feelings and resentments; power imbalance and inequality; illness and anxiety, or sexual attraction directed outside of the relationship in an affair. Life and work impinge on our freedoms; we have to take on responsibilities and feelings of love and sexual interest can get separated. Some couples end up being roommates, loving each other but without sexual interest. For others, one may retain sexual interest, but love and respect can be missing. They go through the motions, wanting the sensuality of sex but not feeling connected to their partner in the same loving way. The open vulnerability of loving feelings and thoughts change. Hurt, anger and disappointment from conflict and disagreement can harden our hearts. The desire that once wanted us to acclaim our love by shouting from the rooftops has now fled. Our thoughts tell us of all the wrongs that have been done to us by our lover and our feelings become concealed in a hard shell.

Sexual styles

There are three different sexual styles as defined by the researcher and psychologist Donald L Mosher. Our sexual style is how we interact sexually with our partner. Some of this is learned from media and porn but it is also about our character and personality. We have adapted Mosher's work and defined the styles as: partner-focused, self-focused and connection-focused. We're likely to have a preference for one of these above the others and, in the ever-changing nature of being human, at different times of our life, in different situations and with different partners, we'll adopt different sexual styles.

Changing your sexual style is about where you put your attention, either on yourself, your partner or the interactions between you. As a relationship develops, the sexual style between partners will change as partners become more comfortable with each other. As this happens sexual styles can be chosen more freely and there can be more fluidity in sexual interactions. It is also possible to get stuck in one sexual style over another and practicing moving to a different style can help move through sexual difficulties. Partner-focused and self-focused sexual styles derive pleasure from different routes. If you get pleasure primarily from seeing your partner having pleasure, that's the indirect route of pleasure found in the partner-focused sexual style. A direct route of pleasure is found in the self-focused style when the person is focused on their own bodily sensations or fantasies. Often we will be using both of them simultaneously. But we usually have a preference for one over the other, so it is useful to bring awareness to how we actually get aroused. If you're bored or turned off by the idea of sex with your partner, try a different interactional sexual style. If sex feels disconnecting or lacking intimacy it could be because you are stuck in the self-focused sexual style. Like a cat that likes to lie in the sunshine, humans are pleasure seeking. We want to bask in the sunshine, to feel softness on our skin, to taste the sweetness of life's fruits. But how we get pleasure and become aroused is dependent not just on the physical stimulation, but also on what we give attention to and the meaning we make of it.

Self-focused

This style derives arousal foremost from bodily sensation in physical contact through touch. You might have your eyes closed or be in a dark room and are directly stimulated through the body with your own or someone else's touch. The self-focused arousal style uses mostly the direct route of pleasure. The person who is self-focused during sexual activity will often have their eyes closed to maximise the awareness of sensations. There will be minimal or no talking so that the sensations of pleasure are all-engrossing.

This style is about staying in the zone, tracking arousal, focusing on sensations in the body and soaking in satisfaction. When this goes well, being absorbed in sensuality is like a trance, an altered state of consciousness. Problems can arise with this arousal style, because what brings us physical pleasure one moment can be dull or boring the next. For instance our mind has drifted to thinking about the meeting tomorrow at work or who is in the bedroom next door. Where we put our attention directly correlates with the amount of pleasure we are able to feel. As does the meaning we make of it. If, for some reason, we are not in a good place emotionally or physically with ourselves or our partner, then whatever we do will not produce the right results, even if we pour all our attention onto it. Another difficulty that can arise with this style is when one partner feels used by the other, when it becomes all about the other's pleasure and they don't get anything out of it. What brings one person desire is another person's disgust. When it doesn't go well the heightened vulnerability can cause resistance, embarrassment or shame.

Partner-focused

Getting turned on by seeing your partner experience sexual pleasure in response to what you are doing with them is known as the indirect route of pleasure. In partner-focused arousal, pleasure is derived from seeing your partner having pleasure. You are stimulated by what you see through the visual pathway, and when that matches the sexual template in your mind it causes sexual arousal. Physical touch might be secondary. Some people with a partner-focused arousal style can have an orgasm through indirect pleasure without any direct physical touch. If this is your arousal style, you are turned on by seeing your partner in an aesthetic way, appreciating the soft curves or rippling muscles of their naked body. You might also enjoy seeing them wear sexy clothing or watching them moving provocatively for your pleasure. You delight in giving them sexual touch and being witness to them getting turned on.

Culturally, there's strong conditioning towards the indirect route of pleasure through the visual senses and the influence of the beauty industry, advertising, porn and media. The difficulty is that this style can put too much pressure on the other partner. They can be made responsible for turning their partner on and this can be difficult to sustain. Some partners can feel they are on a pedestal and are idealised as a fantasy, unrecognised as a real person.

Connection-focused

The connection-focused arousal style is found when partners turn towards each other and engage in eye contact, conversation and play. This style uses both indirect and direct routes of pleasure, filling the space between you in playful exchange of seeing and being seen by each other, touching, talking and fantasy role play. Partners with this arousal style captivate each other emotionally, disclosing private truths to help build their unique interrelatedness. Some experience a blurring of the boundary between them physically and emotionally. Lovemaking for this style can become a playground for impromptu theatre when each sees the other in different roles and acts them out. This might include the players co-ordinating with the setting, costumes and props. You may shop together for sex toys, books, lingerie and so on. You may create an actual pick-up scene at a restaurant or club and take them back home or to a hotel. Role play is fun and exciting, though also perhaps scary to play out or go along with the range of each other's ideas.

The connection-focused style is potentially deeply liberating and can bring arousing complexity and connection to your sexual relationship but can also be challenging. When this goes well, sex feels like surrendering to connection with your partner and beyond. When it doesn't go well, it may be that one person isn't willing to 'show up' and face the vulnerability of being seen at this level.

Who is the pleasure for?

Sometimes we might want to give pleasure to our partner and at other times, we might want to take pleasure from them.

But if reciprocal exchange becomes a bargaining currency, turn-taking can be tiresome and boring. The 'I've done this for you, so you must do this for me' is a big turn-off.

In these days of greater awareness around sexual exploitation and abuse, sexual 'taking' has become synonymous with abusive behaviour. But taking can be a sexual pleasure if you know that your partner is willingly allowing you to do so. Betty Martin has elucidated this beautifully in her 'Wheel of Consent'. So often, our sexual relationships do not start with communication and clarity of who is the pleasure for, and therefore there is no consent. Being able to give consent requires partners to be able to voice what they want and what they will and will not be happy doing in the bedroom.

Bringing awareness to the question of who the pleasure is for can relieve the burden of ambiguity and doubt. Then it becomes a question of communicating consent and creating clarity over who is giving and who is accepting, or who is allowing and who is taking. For example, in an activity involving non-sexual touch like a sports massage, it is clear that the benefit is for the person receiving the massage. The person giving the massage is offering touch in service to the one receiving it. The one receiving it is directing the touch, saying how they would like to be touched. They might have aching muscles in their shoulders and it is a great benefit and pleasure to have them massaged. However, if the masseur's hands meander down from their shoulders and start massaging their back and buttocks when the client has said they want their shoulders massaged, the masseur is no longer in service, they have transgressed this agreement. The massage was for their client, but this is reversed when the pleasure becomes theirs.

Consider another scenario: two people are in a reciprocal erotic situation, but without clear parameters of who is giving and who is receiving. One partner is stroking their partner's back, thinking they like it. The partner having their back stroked thinks their partner is enjoying themselves. It could be that both partners are enjoying the activity or that they are both enduring it because they think that the other is enjoying themselves. When things get more intimate and steamier, patting, rubbing, licking, or sucking parts of the body, it is important to be clear; who is this for? If I get great pleasure in stroking my partner's back, I can ask them if they are willing for me to enjoy their body in this way. If they say yes and the stroking goes ahead, it may be that they get pleasure from it too, or they get indirect pleasure from knowing I am enjoying their body.

So often, our sexual relationships do not start with communication and clarity of who is the pleasure for, and this is problematic. It could be that both people think the other is enjoying themselves, and so both endure an activity, thinking they are being generous. Whereas, in fact, the generous act would be to pause and reconnect and check with them. Another issue is that there is no consent. Being able to give consent requires partners to be able to voice what they want and what they will and will not be happy doing in a sexual situation.

The role of fantasy

Fantasies are a big part of a sexual relationship and can help a couple to see each other as sexual beings again in the humdrum of domestic life. The psychoanalyst Stephen

Mitchell said that fantasy is the handmaiden of desire. Without fantasy, imagination and dreams, desire dies.

Fantasy can certainly be a powerful aphrodisiac. It can also lead to disappointment when the physical reality turns out to be something completely different from what we imagined. Pornography is readily available for a quick turn-on. Yet the mechanics, messiness and complexities of real sex can turn out to be more of a turn-off. Our private fantasies can be far more reliable a turn-on than the reality of experience. We may even remain in our world of fantasy while engaging in sex, which can be part of how we arouse ourselves. It's called subjective arousal, when our mind is a major contributor to physical arousal. Fantasy can be safer than risking disappointment. It's not unusual to go to bed with someone else while also engaging with a fantasy element in your mind during sex. The mind is the most erotic organ.

Fantasy and imagination are defining characteristics of being human. We can imagine and fantasise about the life we want, the job we want, the food we want and the sex we want. Being able to visualise is important in generating motivation and being able to meet our life goals. But it's a fine balance. Reality rarely matches the mind's image. In sexual relationships, this can lead to disappointment as well as performance anxiety before a sexual encounter. For some people, it can be difficult to imagine their partner as sexy after they've been breastfeeding the baby. Or after you're both exhausted from doing chores all day long. We need to create space within ourselves for fantasy and imagination to stimulate our arousal and life force. It's that tension between the familiar and the novel again.

But, used in the wrong way, fantasy can split a couple, too. For instance, one partner may turn to pornography in the quest to find the life-giving force of arousal. What is attractive in porn is what we project onto it from our own fantasy life. We insert ourselves into an imaginary world. But it can take the desire out of the relational space between you.

Knowing your partner, or thinking you know them, can be perilous for eroticism. It's a paradox that we want to know our partner, to make our lives more stable and predictable, yet once we have done this, it tends to kill off the desire to stay with them. Something known becomes stultifying and dull. At times, we yearn for the new and fresh, for someone we don't know. Seeking out the new is often erotically charged because we make it so. A little anxiety can help with arousal and excitement. However, too much can make it impossible to enjoy sex at all.

Wanting versus willing

There is an important difference between willing and wanting. Being willing means we agree to something or are ready to do something; wanting means we desire something, perhaps something we lack. If you want a cup of tea you may be willing to get up and make yourself one, to satisfy your want, or maybe not. You may ask somebody else, 'Would you be willing to make me a cup of tea?', and they can either say yes or no. If you ask them, 'Do you want to make me a cup of tea?' what we're usually actually asking is, 'Are you willing to make me a cup of tea?'

One partner might want sex, and they want the other partner to want sex, but they don't. However, their partner may still be willing. Just because they don't feel spontaneous desire that doesn't necessarily mean they don't want to get into a sexy situation, which may well lead to them wanting sex. One partner may be aware that they usually enjoy sex and feel it is good for the relationship and for bonding, even if they wouldn't describe themselves as 'wanting sex' very often.

A willing partner is often underrated, as if they're substandard, their desire is lacking, their libido needs repair as if they have to be coerced into the sexy situation. This is incorrect, divisive and destructive. A willing partner is willing, and that is a massive difference from being unwilling. Of course, we all want to be wanted, to be desired, to be longed for, like it is in the movies. Real life is more nuanced, more subtle. Desire is complex and willingness is a beautiful state to be in.

In our consumer culture, we are used to throwing things away when they don't work instead of repairing them. Likewise, we often think our relationship is over if we don't get what we want or we don't feel highly sexually attracted to our partner all the time. However, real life is much more nuanced – it is always possible to work on sexual desire with your partner, trying new things and creating new life in the relationship. Sometimes sex is something that requires effort – connecting with our partner's desires and wants to find new ways for you to experiment.

It is always important to check in with ourselves before sex, on every level. Perhaps our mind is saying, 'I'm tired, I'm stressed, there's not enough time, I'm annoyed at you, I'm depleted and want some quiet time.' But when we look into our heart, despite the external pressures, it might be that you do indeed want to connect with your partner sexually. It's important to consider what you really want.

When we understand differences in the way we get turned on – particularly differences between contextual and spontaneous desire – it can help us to feel OK about ourselves and our own desire. It need not be shaming. We can then make a bridge from our own position to our partner. This will probably involve more conversation around what works and what doesn't for each of you and what you would like from your sexual relationship and each other.

DAVID AND PAT

Asking for sex is difficult for David because he experiences shame around having sexual longings. He feels vulnerable and uncomfortable, so he asks as infrequently as he can bear, hoping that Pat notices they haven't had sex in a while and initiates something. But Pat doesn't have spontaneous desire like David and so sex doesn't enter her mind. After several weeks, David will eventually ask for sex but, by this point, he cannot conceal his frustration. Because of his pent-up irritation with Pat, she hears his suggestion as a demand on her, something she doesn't respond well to. She's already feeling overwhelmed with too much to do: she's had a busy day at work, she's got many things on her 'to-do' list, so this just sounds like another burden. 'If you want an orgasm, why don't you go and masturbate?' she says impatiently. Because he asks so seldom, this rejection feels painful to David. He feels misunderstood and angry. He emotionally withdraws, leaving Pat feeling abandoned. She is less able to ask him for what she wants now because of his mood. Now she feels angry and alone.

What David didn't know before he withdrew in anger is that Pat would have been interested in receiving rather than giving. If he offered her something lovely, if he seduced her into something that felt nourishing rather than depleting, things might look different to her. Pat secretly hopes David will take care of her by providing the context for her to feel sexy and wanted. She knows that she has contextual arousal and needs to be in the right place. She would like a full body massage to help her unwind and would be interested if it turned into an erotic massage. But instead of expecting David to know what she wants, Pat must take responsibility for communicating her wishes directly. And David must manage his feelings of vulnerability and shame about asking for sex.

David can't ask Pat for sex because it's too risky for him to expose any sexual desire on his part. Pat can't ask either for fear of getting into something she might not really want. In some instances, people can shut down their desire or deny it and instead get irritable and angry. In other cases, one partner wants to be wanted without having to put in any effort of their own in order to keep themselves safe from any possible rejection.

ANGELA AND STACY

Asking for sex can be so shameful for some people that they'll resort to oblique forms of communication to get around the problem. Angela and Stacy have had the day off in their holiday cottage. That evening, Angela says: 'Have you achieved everything you wanted to today?' Stacy is perplexed. What does she mean? After several minutes of trying to work it out and then noticing Angela's body language, which screams disappointment, she eventually guesses. Angela wants her to ask her for sex! In not asking for what she wants, Angela is being passive. Passivity and shyness is frustrating for Angela and is a turn-off for Stacy.

When they first met, Angela was a virgin. Stacy initially found this a turn-on; she was her first sexual partner and got a buzz from teaching Angela about the pleasure of sex. But gradually, as their relationship matured, Angela's shyness started to inhibit their sexual activity in the bedroom. Stacy resents being her sexual tutor and it becames a turn-off for her. She wants a more symmetrical relationship. If Angela learns to be more self-confident and take authority by asking for what she wants and being assertive in the bedroom, this will be a turn-on for Stacy, giving her permission to reciprocate.

Asking for, accepting and rejecting sexual contact

It can be useful to make the distinction between a question that begins 'Can I . . .?' or 'May I . . .?' and a question that begins 'Will you . . . ?'. Asking your partner, 'Can I give you an erotic massage tonight?' is asking them if you can take some action towards them. You are the 'doer' and they will be the recipient. If you ask, 'Will you come and give me a hug?', you are asking them to be the doer and you the recipient. Healthy sexual and intimate relationships depend on the autonomy of the partners to be able to ask clearly and unambiguously for what they want to do or have done to them; for each partner to freely respond with a 'yes' or a 'no' and for each partner to tolerate some degree of rejection. Saying yes and no is fundamental, as we discussed in Chapter Four on boundaries: we need to be able to accept or reject. If we can't do one or the other, the value of both is depreciated. Saying yes to sex and then not being able to enjoy it or be fully present in the experience would not be satisfying to either partner.

Experiencing intense sexual desire with our partners that is not being met can provoke high anxiety for many people. The person who wants something from their partner perceives themselves to be in a vulnerable position because they depend on the other to satisfy their sexual longings. It can be excruciating to long for something and feel powerless in satisfying your desires and painful to know that the desire we feel for our partner is not mirrored and directed back at us. It feels like a rejection.

We all know what it's like to get rejected. And we know how much it hurts, a stinging, sore, festering feeling. We avoid it at all costs, by people pleasing, negating our desires, making ourselves small and trying to fit in. It can also feel deeply shameful to be rejected, particularly by our partner – we can take it as a judgement on our very existence, rather than information about the person who has rejected us. Our need to belong, to fit in, to be included and loved for who we are is such a core need. When we offer something and it is not accepted, resentments can build and we harbour hurt feelings and negative thoughts. Nowhere is this truer than in the bedroom.

Looking at the attachment styles of Pat and David, Pat is the 'turtle' and David the 'octopus'. He is the one to reach out and want more closeness and intimacy; he seeks comfort and reassurance through hearing how much he is needed. Pat is the one who wants more space. She seeks refuge in her solitude, where she can recharge. She feels respected by being given space and left alone. If they don't communicate fully, they reach an impasse. Pat says 'no' and David feels deeply rejected. If they stay in contact and communicate well, Pat may be able to give David a timeframe, to frame her 'no' into postponement: 'Right now, I just need some time on my own but I can be with you in an hour.' Or, 'I really enjoy sex with you, but I've had a lousy day at work and I just want to watch TV, can we schedule it for tomorrow?' That way, David doesn't have to take the rejection as an absolute 'no'; he and Pat remain in connection and both can take care of their needs, knowing that they will come together soon. Pat is showing David that she is motivated towards the relationship and towards getting turned on with him. Scheduling sex, particularly in long-term relationships, can be a really beneficial way of creating structure and boundaries around desire.

When we accept, we take something into ourselves and we assume responsibility for taking it. Resting in the flow of experience without resistance can open new ways of managing events, feelings and situations, and gives us a sense of responsibility and empowerment. It doesn't mean that we don't have any negative emotions, such as anger, disappointment or sadness. It just means that we feel them and then work through them.

Our story

In the years after the babies were born, and the time after one of the twins died, we didn't have sex that often. Our sex life became a catalyst for grief, despair and disappointment. It stirred anger and sadness as we remembered the dreams of our future and experienced a sense that our bodies had failed us, each other and one of our babies. In the following years, we tried to conceive again, through the fertility clinic, which resulted in miscarriages and failed conceptions. It was an immensely difficult time, testing us in different ways. Eventually, we came to a decision to stop trying to have more children. We decided that we'd tried enough and had reached our limit, and were glad to stop and be grateful for the child we did have.

Arguing about sex isn't quite like any other kind of argument. It was painfully vulnerable, exposing and hurtful to be putting our precious, harmonious and unifying sex life through the mincer by bickering about it and disputing it. The arguments we fell into were, on the surface, about when. Sex needed planning and preparation. This is the right time. This is not the right time. Arguments wore us down. Other arguments, about unrelated topics, would seem to gravitate back to this argument. We called it our 'hamster wheel' because we would go round and round familiar territory, getting nowhere.

We both wanted to feel wanted, we both wanted the closeness and intimacy of sexual contact, but neither of us were mature enough to manage how and when to approach the other. We read books about sex and relationships and tried many exercises and techniques. We went to workshops and saw a couples' therapist. Each approach would help for a while and then we'd return to our hamster wheel. We knew that many couples have a similar impasse, that the sordid battleground is familiar to many.

It changed imperceptibly slowly. At some point, we shifted into a new chapter, where we seemed to arrive in a sexier place. The battleground dissolved; we put down our swords and shields. What exactly made the change was no one specific thing, it was all of it. All the work we were doing on ourselves, the workshops, the training separately and together, the exercises, the healing journey, the therapy – it all added up and we were both supported enough to be able to come to mutual understanding of each other.

Sexually, that opened up a new phase. Conceiving more children was off the agenda, which left sex as a place of meeting each other anew, for pleasure, for sensuality, to treat ourselves and each other kindly. Sex for lovemaking, for sacred sensual celebration, for intimate time together. Sex as a playground, as a private profound experience and as a way to heal our hurt hearts.

What's it like to have sex with the same person for 25 years? When we were young this would have seemed too strange a thought. Did people actually have sex past the age of 50? If they did, it surely can't be much of a turn-on. Yet, the opposite is true: we have greater capacity for intimacy and we are more able to say what we want, to speak preferences that would have embarrassed us or felt too exposing when we were young. We have built a great trust. We're less shy, more relaxed; we see each other and enjoy being seen for the whole of who we are. We don't need sex, but we get some of our needs met through sex:

needs for play, excitement, or risk taking; needs for caring, sensuality or reciprocal respect. And there's a sense that we cannot take each other for granted. Our bodies, ever-changing – how will they be in years ahead? This is all we have, now. We adapt and our idea of what lovemaking is changes in multiple creative ways.

Exercises

Three-minute Game

The 3-Minute Game is offered here with grateful thanks to Betty Martin, who we both trained with. She devised the game and the Wheel of Consent and gave us permission to use it here. This game is based on these two simple questions:

1. How would you like me to touch you for three minutes?
2. How would you like to touch me for three minutes?

Decide who is partner one and who is partner two. Partner one asks partner two, 'How would you like me to touch you for three minutes?' Partner two has to think what they would most like and tell the other. For some people, it is difficult to receive touch and they may not know what they would like. It is important that partner one considers the answer they get and decides if they are willing to give the touch that has been requested. They may want to ask more questions, to clarify something about the request, or they may want to make limits to feel comfortable. When the touch has been agreed, partner one gives the touch requested with any agreed changes to partner two for three minutes.

When the three minutes has ended, partner one asks the second question to partner two: 'How would you like to touch me for three minutes?' With this question, partner one is offering their body to be touched in a way that partner two would like to touch it for their own pleasure. The answer has to be carefully considered by partner one to ensure they are happy to give consent for their partner to touch their body in the requested way for three minutes. If there are any limits or changes on the request, these should be discussed before the three minutes starts. When three minutes has elapsed, the roles are reversed and partner two asks partner one, 'How would you like me to touch you for three minutes?'

It's important to remember that during the three minutes, either partner can at any time renegotiate the terms of the touch being given or received. You can say if something is not right for you as you go along and get an adjustment that's comfortable for you. This is an important lesson for sexual relationships and in life generally. You can always change your mind.

What can go wrong?

The 3-Minute Game could seem mechanical if you are not really engaged in a joyous way. So try to ensure that you give and receive with a full heart.

It may feel difficult to take overt pleasure from your partner's body and this can give rise to feelings of guilt or shame. Instead of getting stuck there, take this as useful information about yourself. Most of us are far more comfortable in giving pleasure as a service instead of taking pleasure.

What can go well?

You have fun and are clear with each other, enjoying giving and taking. You might learn what you find easy or more difficult. Maybe you are better at accepting touch than offering touch for your own pleasure? Or the other way round? It is useful to have at least a few rounds of the game so you can experience giving and receiving consent within the safety of a defined frame.

Scheduling dates and sex

Scheduling dates for sex can sound a bit, well, unsexy. We like to think of sex happening in the spur of the moment, in the throes of passion, like in the movies. And it may well do, particularly in a new relationship. But in a longer relationship, there can be both time limitations and inclination limitations on sex: the demands of busy work and family life inevitably results in time for lovemaking becoming a topic of tension. The higher-desire partner will expect the lower-desire partner to have the same libido drive as them and can be frustrated when they don't. Scheduling regular dates for sex is reassuring for both, as it can take a lot of stress out of uncertainty and waiting. Importantly, scheduling sex signals willingness for an erotic encounter. This parallels the dating experience of new couples at the outset of their relationship when a date would be looked forward to and sex anticipated.

However, scheduling a date to work for your diary doesn't mean you'll definitely be in the mood when the time comes, but it's important to show up and be willing and curious if you can be. It is OK to alter arrangements or make creative adjustments if you do not feel like having sex. Sexual arousal occurs for people in different ways, either spontaneous or contextual. People with spontaneous arousal are those who are aware of feeling turned on and look to get themselves in a sexy situation. Those who are contextually aroused won't necessarily feel turned on until they are in a sexy situation. Once in the right context, doing the right things, their arousal will ignite. Scheduling dates allows the couple to be a sexy couple, not only a couple who has sex. Time outside the schedule can be flirtatious, cuddly and playful for its own sake, rather than an ambiguous preamble for seduction.

10

How to Build Love

What is love?

This book is about how to build a relationship – and not just any relationship but an intimate relationship, one where both partners can thrive as individuals and as a couple while sustaining their love and desire for one another. We have described the building blocks of the relationship and how to work together so that the third body, that space between you that has its own life, can flourish and grow.

But why commit to having an intimate relationship at all, you might ask. Couples get together and commit to stay together for many reasons: security, the sense of family and belonging, the desire for children and also for sex. But for the majority of people who are reading this book, the purpose of a relationship will be to find and share a special kind of love with another human being. Love gives life meaning; it allows us to find the best parts of ourselves and live life more fully. A life full of love is a life well lived.

We have a sense of what love feels like, and we all long for that love, but most of us don't really know what love is, beyond how we experience it, nor do we know how to find it. Secular Western culture sends us messages that the love we are looking for is romantic – the happily ever after. That to love and be loved by a partner will fill our emotional holes, fix all our problems and make us happy. Most of us on some level still believe that this is a worthy dream to chase after, which is why we spend so much time searching for the perfect other, but we also know that this is usually not how things work out. That degree of fairytale perfection does not match up with reality.

For those people who are lucky enough to find the potential for love, how do we sustain it? That is what this book has been about – not just about how to build a relationship, but how to build love. Love as a feeling is intoxicating but it will come and go. To be sustained, love has to be generated between you. Love is alive only when we feed and keep it alive with our actions, over and over again. If we don't do this, the love will die. As bell hooks, the author and social activist, said: 'But love is really more of an interactive process. It's about what we do not just what we feel. It's a verb, not a noun.' Love is active, and it takes both practice and courage.

Love is more than a feeling

When we fall in love, we bond. We expand our heart to incorporate the other, to meet in the space between, which becomes dynamic as our separateness falls away. A type of alchemical merging happens when we let the other in but the individuals remain intact. Communication is alive in the field between us. Love is the catalyst, the ingredient that creates the bridge between our two islands.

As outlined earlier in the book, love is often associated with the euphoric feelings identified within the first two years of a romantic relationship. Often referred to as 'falling in love', this phase is marked by infatuation with the idea of the loved one. We are passionately driven towards seeing them and being with them. We can't stop thinking about them. There is something uncontrollable about falling in love. It is as if it is beyond our own volition, as if it is just happening to us. Lovers spin fairytales together and create infectious energy through mutual passion. Erotic fantasy can be obsessional. This is the frenzy of 'falling in love'.

The love that we fall into, that overcomes us and takes us to a place of euphoria, is the love that lights up all parts of us: our thoughts, feelings, impulses and felt sense of ourselves as embodied beings. All these functions within us are changed, even transformed. It's as if we are charmed like a snake from the basket by the tune our lover is playing on their magic flute. Often these feelings are so intoxicating that people experience a loss of appetite, anxiety and difficulty concentrating and sleeping. But it's only temporary.

After the honeymoon of love's blindness, we are awakened from our hypnotised state. The warmth of the candlelight is gone and we see our partner in the cold light of day. The effects of the emotional cocktail wear off, sometimes leaving us feeling disillusioned with the idea that love is possible. Ultimately, it fails to deliver the long-term fix we were looking for. This is why some people fall in love with love itself and give up on a relationship when the 'in love' feelings seep away. They are exhilarated by the experience of romantic love and the feelings it generates and so seek another new relationship to deliver the chemical fix of being with the fantasy of a near-perfect person.

The initial romantic feelings are just the launch pad for the relationship. When they fade, we are left to take up the challenge of love. This is the work of relationship – to deliver love through our own volition. A decision has to be made to commit to loving one another. Love is an active choice that must have autonomy to survive. It requires a free choice to let it in and needs space to live. We are shown the charms of love to help us on our way to turning love into action and creating the relationship.

Love is made by us

Love generates a warm golden glow of feelings inside of us, but love is not the same as these feelings. Once created, love is a force that exists independently of the feelings it can generate. Like nature, basic goodness, or sunshine, it is just there, but it needs our loving intention, attention and action to draw it to us. Through the willingness to take loving actions in an intimate relationship, the space between you in a couple relationship becomes the home for love, where it takes up residence and lives as the third body between you.

Love needs us to bring it into our relationships. It is not merely a feeling. We learn to love by doing things for each other, giving attention, time and energy to the relationship. We demonstrate love so it becomes tangible and visible. While we may have been idolising each other at the beginning of the relationship, this means stepping out into the daylight and taking responsibility for your own wants and needs, and asking for help when it is required. Healthy inter-dependence is being able to ask for what you need or want from your partner in a mature adult way and being able to manage if they can't meet your wants or needs in that moment. Inter-dependence is being able to hold the tension between the polarities of complete dependence and self-sufficiency. When both partners in the relationship can recognise this place, commitment can begin and a second phase of loving is initiated.

Hidden in the disappointment of the loss of the honeymoon phase of the relationship is the opportunity for our own evolution and growth. We don't only make relationships; relationships make us. For those couples who choose to commit to this next stage, the work of allowing the relationship to make you begins. This is the richly rewarding yet also risky path of relationship.

The social psychologist Erich Fromm said love is work. It is a state that requires discipline, concentration and patience. Feelings are fickle. They come and go. Love is what we do and how we behave towards our partner. As bell hooks said, love is a verb, demonstrated through action. Love is trustworthy and enduring.

Love as fusion and separation

The polarity of fusion and separation is one of the fundamental movements in a relationship. Love propels us towards fusion and gives us the courage to overcome differences and find similarities. The paradox is that we love another *because* of their difference and individuality. So the one tends to negate the other. Being stuck in fusion will obliterate the space between you because there is no room for air to circulate. The third body, the dynamic between you, needs to breathe.

The challenge of love is to balance the two opposing forces of fusion and separation. The space between you is the balancing chamber, into which each person can move freely and be welcomed as a visitor. Both of you must take responsibility for keeping it alive.

If we love, we can also hate

The polarity of love is hate. We cannot know about love unless we understand the meaning of hate. Loving and hating can be seen as movements either towards or away. We move towards those things we love and move away from the things we hate. It's a basic survival mechanism. We look for comfort and ease and we move away from discomfort and unease. At a primitive level, we are always scanning for danger. Will this person hurt me or be kind to me? Will they keep my heart safe? We need to know this in our quest to feel safe and comfortable. This knowing is a whole body activity that happens below conscious awareness. We read an expression on someone's face, for instance, or it's the tone of their voice; we notice they fold their arms, have their hands in their pockets or drop eye contact as they speak to us. We receive these signals and create a message from them. But our triggers are not always reliable. Maybe that person was anxious, stressed or scared? And we read the fear on their face and mistook it for preoccupation, arrogance or aggression. Love is the generosity to see beyond your partner's imperfections, to be forgiving and kind and to allow them the benefit of the doubt. It is the willingness to understand them and their difficulties.

Love and hate are two sides of the same coin. To love someone means we can also hate them as well. The coin can flip at any moment and love can turn into its opposite. The act of love requires vulnerability, to allow ourselves to be fully in contact with another. This renders us vulnerable to riskier reactions and intense emotions that we would prefer not to have – disgust, disappointment, shame and grief. We cannot avoid these entirely, as a heart that chooses to love is open to the whole kaleidoscope of human feeling.

As we explained in Chapter Six in the discussion on polarities, polar opposites have something in common, are held in tension and inform each other. In the case of love and hate, both create an intense connection to their source – one attracting, the other repelling. These related forces of attraction are also found in sympathy and antipathy, and liking and disliking; where one draws us close, the other averts us. You can't have one without the other as they are contrasting modes of a single phenomenon.

The psychologist Wilhelm Stekel recognised in 1921 that there is no love without hate and no hate without love. He observed that 'love and hate must go hand in hand; and the people we love most we hate also, because hate is grounded in the nature of love.' This is the true nature of a polarity, that the other side exists simultaneously and that one defines the other.

Absence of love in apathy and indifference

We have been speaking about the polar opposite of love. But it is important to recognise there is also what is known as a logical opposite, which is its absence – 'not love'. Stekel called the absence of love indifference and the psychologist Rollo May called it apathy. Apathy is the absence of will and is thus devoid of either caring or loathing. We have seen how love is an active principle, so will is essential for love. Where there is no will, there is apathy and hence no love, because will is the necessary volitional force to carry us through adversity to love and be responsible in our loving. Scott Peck describes love as the will to extend one's self for the purpose of nurturing one's own or another's spiritual growth. The antecedent of love is this interest in others over ourselves. Rudolf Steiner describes love as a creative force which is selfless and can overcome egoism.

Apathy and indifference are devoid of the will to find volition to be creative, to be curious, to reach out and connect and ultimately to practise the activity of loving. So when a couple enters a state of indifference, the relationship is in serious jeopardy. This can happen when one or both partners close down emotionally and withdraw the connection to protect themselves from further hurt and disappointment. Being in a state of fighting and hating is still to be in connection. The writer, George Bernard Shaw, believed, 'The worst sin towards our fellow creatures is not to hate them, but to be indifferent to them: that's the essence of inhumanity.' Indifference is the antithesis of love and is a completely different state. As human beings, we have the potential to be loving instead of indifferent. That means finding the will for volitional relating in love. This is a love which is transpersonal, not given for, nor expecting egoistic gratification. It is love of a new order above the dichotomy of love and hate. It can see the true person behind their traits and behaviour and has compassion for their emotional wounds and struggles.

Love is freedom and responsibility

Love means taking responsibility for our own development as only we can know what is most important to us. While we may have been looking after each other in more infantile ways, this is a time to look after ourselves and take responsibility for meeting some of our own needs. This is the polarity inherent in active loving. We need to love ourselves, to take responsibility for what we want out of life, as well as loving our partner and helping them to evolve.

In having self-worth and self-compassion, you attract love to you because you have confidence in your lovability. If you can only love yourself because someone else loves you, you make yourself dependent on that love. It's like saying, 'I only love myself if you love me' or 'I'm only worthy if you think I'm worthy'. Or if you say, 'I'm happy if you're happy', you are making the other person responsible for your happiness. Neither you nor your partner can be free if you depend on them for their love. Loving our partner from a place of volition takes us to a feeling of unity with the world and everything and everyone in it.

Love lives in freedom: the freedom to choose. Love has to be freely given. Initially, when we fall in love, it is involuntary. Later we choose it; we make the conscious decision to continue, to commit, to voluntarily stay in the relationship. Love cannot be demanded or given on demand. For love to thrive in the third body between you, there must be equal respect and recognition of each other as an independent person and validation of their contribution to the relationship.

Freedom, choice and responsibility go together. You can't have one without the other. The implications of loving someone are great. Loving another requires us to be responsible, to some extent, for the one we love. If we take our freedom to choose love then immediately we are faced with responsibility for that choice. This can require sacrifice and hard work. Sometimes when we love we also have to accept saying no in a loving and responsible way. If you shun responsibility, you cannot truly enjoy freedom.

Love takes practice

Discipline is not control, it isn't a cage, it's a springboard. It's holding your boundaries securely enough to be spontaneous. Being safe enough to be dangerous. Discipline is the ability to set your focus or to change habits that no longer serve their purpose. Perhaps we mindlessly scroll on our phones, binge watch TV, have another drink or another of the many ways we numb ourselves without consciously choosing to spend our lives this way, without pausing to ask, what is truly satisfying? What nourishes us on a deeper level? How do we choose to live? Discipline becomes an act of supreme kindness as we make choices to break out of the mould.

There is great joy in choosing the freedom and responsibility of loving well and spreading love in the world from the heart of your relationship to others around you. This requires taking the freedom to respond to your partner with love from a place of awareness and choice, rather than a place of reaction and programming from the past. This is being responsible, being present and aware.

Is there such a thing as free will? How much choice do we have over our lives? Sometimes life happens to us and we do not choose those things that are painful or difficult. But we do have choice over the meaning we give to things that happen and how we respond, however painful. We choose our values and our philosophical outlook. What meaning we make of things, how we think of things and how we feel about what happens in our lives is ours to choose. The same is true in relationships. We can choose whether we react angrily to our partner or whether to respond with care.

Your partner was chosen by you. Even in an arranged marriage, your heart can choose to accept them or reject them. It's your choice, not a random game of chance. Every choice requires an exclusion of others. To choose one's partner is to deny others, unless you have an open relationship or are polyamorous. To be authentic, one must offer the same freedom to your partner as you would yourself. Which means that if you want other partners, you must accept that they might want the same.

Some couples come to therapy and say they don't love their partner anymore. They have fallen out of love and just don't 'feel it' any more. Although it feels as if it just happened to us, falling out of love is actually choosing not to love. The partner who is 'not feeling it' has turned their attention to other things – maybe to another person, or the idea of another person and relationship, or work, or friends. They have, consciously or unconsciously, chosen to turn away and look elsewhere. Or they focus on parts of the partner they dislike, criticise or disapprove of, which fuels and legitimises their feelings that their partner is now unlovable.

If your partner behaves in ways that you find difficult, it is important you tell them what would work better for you. Doing this is loving in itself. It is a loving act to tell someone what you need, want or desire. This is the process of moving from the idealised 'falling in love stage' to the enduring 'standing in love'. It takes courage to speak out and open yourself in a loving way to your partner. It is courageous, as it reveals something about you, your preferences that come through in your request. This means you don't blame them, you just state what it is that bothers you and what you need instead.

When you enter periods of difficulty in your relationship, it can be easy to see other potential partners as problem-free alternatives. You think that they will be a more loving and easier-going partner than the one you have. But the common denominator of all your relationship is you. You carry equal responsibility for the quality of your relationship. Yes, you have the freedom to choose to jump ship and build another relationship, or focus on yourself. And there are circumstances where this would be the best option, such as in abusive relationships. But you also have the freedom to choose this relationship again and to choose your partner again, this time in full awareness, this time knowing that you have partially created them and they you. We can choose to accept our responsibility for how we have created them, put them in a box by labelling them and focusing our disowned polarity attributes onto them. And we can choose to take these back voluntarily. The positive polarities and projections are withdrawn easily enough, but taking responsibility for modifying our own behaviour is more difficult to do. This has to be a free choice. Otherwise, we will stay and resent our partner.

To love and be loved is a practice. Because when we are loved, we might ask: 'Why are we loved?' 'What do I do that deserves this love?' As children, if all goes well, we are loved unconditionally, just as we are. But as adults, the love we receive is based on reciprocal behaviour from our partner. We are not loved for being moody or withdrawn, critical or angry. We are loved for the positive things we do for our partner and the relationship. But we are not being loving when we stop doing loving things or when we choose to hate or to remain dysregulated. An important aspect of loving someone is holding them in our love even when they are withdrawn or critical. We hold the image of them as the loving person we know they can be, keeping them in loving thoughts even when we are not seeing them in a positive light.

To love takes courage

Loving takes the courage to be seen, just as we are. It is the courage to give up our static position and move into the new territory between the extremes of our polar positions. It is the courage to stand alone as an individual and to love yourself and your partner with spaciousness and generosity. To negate your fixed viewpoint and accept another's point of view, which mean empathising and seeing the world from your partner's perspective.

Love is the catalyst, the ingredient that creates the connection. Love manifests in warmth, kindness and compassion in the world, not only from those heroic folk who are pillars in our communities, but small day-to-day actions of many people in daily life. Sweetness, understanding, allowances and generosities. We are, despite it all, optimistic that this ripples out and spreads with the knock-on effect of compassion, goodwill and love. If we are to foster love in the world between neighbours, communities and nations, we must first develop it in our intimate relationships. A relationship is a microcosm of the world; we can build a more loving world, one relationship at a time.

Bibliography

Adrianne Maree Brown - *Pleasure Activism: The Politics of Feeling Good*. AK Press, 2019.

Alice B Stockham & J William Lloyd - *Karezza and the Karezza Method: The Classic Western Approach to Tantric Sexual Healing*. CreateSpace Independent Publishing Platform, 2013.

Barry Johnson - *And: Making a Difference by Leveraging Polarity, Paradox and Dilemma*. Human Resource Development Press, 2020.

Barry Johnson - *Polarity Management, 2nd Edition: Identifying and Managing Unsolvable Problems*. HRD Press, 2014.

Betty Martin - *The Art of Receiving and Giving: The Wheel of Consent*. Luminare Press, 2021.

Brian Emerson & Kelly Lewis - *Navigating Polarities: Using Both/ And Thinking to Lead Transformation*. Paradoxical Press, 2019.

Cloe Madanes - *Relationship Breakthrough*. Harmony/Rodale, 2013.

David Burns - *Feeling Good Together: The secret to making troubled relationships work*. Vermilion, 2009.

David Schnarch - *Passionate Marriage: Keeping Love and Intimacy Alive in Committed Relationships*. W. W. Norton & Company, 2009.

Diana Richardson - *Slow Sex: The Path to Fulfilling and Sustainable Sexuality*. Inner Traditions International, 2011.

Emily Nagorski - *Come as You Are: The surprising new science that will transform your sex life*. Simon & Schuster, 2015.

Erich Fromm - *The Art of Loving*. Thorsons, 1995.

Esther Perel - *Mating in Captivity: How to keep desire and passion alive in long-term relationships*. Hodder & Stoughton, 2006.

Esther Perel - *The State Of Affairs: Rethinking Infidelity – a book for anyone who has ever loved*. Yellow Kite, 2017.

Hal Stone and Sidra Stone – *Embracing Each Other: How to Make All Your Relationships Work for You*. Delos Publications, 1989.

Harville Hendrix and Helen La Kelly Hunt - *Doing Imago Relationship Therapy in the Space-Between: A Clinician's Guide*. W. W. Norton & Company, 2021.

Harville Hendrix - *Getting The Love You Want Revised Edition: A Guide for Couples*. Simon & Schuster UK, 2020.

Helen Fisher – *Anatomy of Love – A Natural History of Mating, Marriage, and Why We Stray*. WW Norton & Co, 2017.

Henri Bortoft - *The Wholeness of Nature: Goethe's Way of Science*. Floris Books, 1996.

Jack Morin - *The Erotic Mind: Unlocking the Inner Sources of Sexual Passion and Fulfilment*. Harper Perennial, 1996.

James Hollis - *The Eden Project: In Search of the Magical Other – Jungian Perspective on Relationship*. Inner City Books, 1998.

Jay Haley - *Problem-Solving Therapy*. Jossey-Bass, 1989.

John Welwood - *Challenge of the Heart: Love, Sex and Intimacy in Changing Times*. Shambhala, 1985.

Leslie A Baxter & Barbara M Montgomery - *Relating: Dialogues and Dialectics*. Guilford Press, 1996.

Marnia Robinson - *Cupid's Poisoned Arrow: From Habit to Harmony in Sexual Relationships*. North Atlantic Books, U.S., 2009.

Michael E. Metz and Barry W. McCarthy: *Enduring Desire: Your Guide to Lifelong Intimacy*. Routledge; 1st edition, 2010.

BIBLIOGRAPHY

Nathaniel Branden - *The Psychology of Romantic Love: Romantic Love in an Anti-Romantic Age.* J P Tarcher/Penguin Putnam. 2008.

Paul Watzlawick , John H. Weakland, et al. *Principles of Problem Formation and Problem Resolution.* W. W. Norton & Co., 2011.

Peggy Kleinplatz - *Magnificent Sex: Lessons from Extraordinary Lovers.* Routledge; 1st edition. 2020.

Robert A Johnson - *We Understanding the Psychology of Romantic Love.*Bravo Ltd; Reprint edition. 1998.

Robert Sternberg & Karin Sternberg (editors) - *The New Psychology of Love.* Yale University Press. 2018.

Sue Johnson - *Hold Me Tight: Your Guide to the Most Successful Approach to Building Loving Relationships.* Piatkus Books. 2011.

Virginia Satir - *The New Peoplemaking.* Science and Behavior Books; 2nd edition. 1989.

Acknowledgements

Thank you to Adam Gauntlett, our literary agent from Peters Fraser & Dunlop, who invited us to write this book. You followed your instinct, reached out and took a chance on us. Thank you to Michelle Signore and Sophie Nevrkla at Bonnier Books, our publisher, for your astute comments and positivity.

Thank you to our son Ry for being so good-natured with our many long hours in the office. Perhaps it was good timing for you, as an older teenager, allowing you to do your own thing. Your maturity and sociability engendered our confidence that you could manage this extra independence.

Piecing together a jigsaw puzzle without the picture on the front of the box is challenging. Our heartfelt thanks goes to Ingrid Yngstrom who was able to take our pieces of writing and rearrange them in such a way that they slotted into place, creating the structure of this book. Ingrid's experience, clear thinking and patient kindness catalysed this writing into a coherent whole. As a developmental editor, reader of the first draft, gestalt psychotherapy trainee alongside Sarah and good friend, Ingrid became our 'third' and brought this project into the logical clarity that it is now.

Many thanks to Andrea Juhan for so much support over so many years, for reading the manuscript and helping us make this what we hope is a better book.

Thank you Betty Martin for your teachings and courses and for allowing us to use some of your exercises and material. Thank you Harville Hendrix and Helen LaKelly Hunt for their Imago training and for allowing us to reference their work.

Thank you to our clients who have graciously allowed us to draw on their stories for this book. We have made composites and fictionalised and anonymised elements, we also changed names and genders, so that no story is directly relatable to any client.

Sarah says: Thank you Matt for being funny and laughing at my jokes and for creating the host of characters/alter egos who popped in to bring comedy into our work together when things got tense. It's a joy to create with you. My gratitude also goes to Sue Rickards for being two steps ahead that I may follow, for your welcoming me to this embodiment work and your warm friendship. I also thank my host of fabulous colleagues at Open Floor, particularly my co-trainers Deborah Lewin and Lucie Nerot who sometimes felt the gap in my contributions to our collective workload while this book was forming.

Matt says: Thanks Sarah for being a wonderful companion, friend, lover, co-worker and co-author. Your patience and good humour made working with you a joy and your brilliant insights light me up in body, soul and spirit. My gratitude to Terry Cooper and the opportunity you offered me at Spectrum which got me started on my training in psychotherapy. I also owe thanks to David Hewison and Tavistock Relationships and the body of knowledge on couple dynamics which I draw on for this book.

Index

INDEX